ANTARCTICA

ANTARCTICA

BEAUTY
IN
THE
EXTREME

JONATHAN CHESTER

Friedman Group

A FRIEDMAN GROUP BOOK

ISBN 1-56138-060-1

ANTARCTICA
Beauty in the Extreme
was prepared and produced by
Michael Friedman Publishing Group, Inc.
15 West 26th Street
New York, New York 10010

Editor: Sharon Kalman
Art Director: Jeff Batzli
Designer: Susan Livingston
Layout: Benjamin Chase
Photography Editor: Christopher C. Bain

All photographs © Jonathan Chester with the following exceptions:
   © Warwick Williams, page 33 top
   © Colin Monteath, pages 47, 48, 126
   © Frank Hurley/Mawson Institute, pages 42, 50, 56

Typeset by The Interface Group
Color separation by Scantrans Pte. Ltd.
Printed and bound in Hong Kong by Leefung-Asco Printers Ltd.

Dedication

To all the pioneers and explorers of the Antarctic,
and to my fellow expeditioners who have shared with me
the wonders of the last great wilderness.

Acknowledgments

I would like to thank Pam Griffiths, Susan Morris-Yates, Quentin Chester, Evan McHugh, and Peter Gill who helped transform my notes and ideas into readable text. Caroline Pope deciphered my handwriting and Jenny Mills and Michelle Havenstein helped with the photo selection.

I would also like to thank Michael Friedman, Karla Olson, Christopher Bain, Sharon Kalman, Dana Rosen, Sue Livingston, and Benjamin Chase for all their support and expertise in bringing this book to fruition.

CONTENTS

INTRODUCTION

Antarctica is breathtaking. Far more than just a cold and inaccessible realm at the bottom of the world, it is an awe-inspiring and exotic land, a place of extremes that cannot fail to make a deep impression.

The southern continent's history, geography, biology, climate, and political status set it apart from the rest of the world. It could be another planet, since humans are unable to survive without complicated trappings from the outside world. NASA has even used Antarctica's dry valleys to test moon vehicles. For those fortunate enough to visit this frozen place, it is an experience of sensory deprivation. It can be so quiet that your own heartbeat rings in your ears. Inland, away from the pungent odor of Adélie penguins, the only smell is that of your own sweat. And it is cold, relentlessly cold. On what passes as a balmy day the temperature will rarely rise above the freezing point. Yet, when the sun is high, the heat and reflected glare can cause snow blindness, dehydration, and sunburn. On an overcast day, the slightest breeze will chill you to the bone. When the weather turns nasty, blizzards can last for weeks and winds howl at hurricane force.

Antarctica is vast, bigger than the United States and Mexico combined. It is regarded by many as the last great wilderness. Although typically depicted as a stark, white, icy void, during the long summer twilight the landscape is often bathed in pink, salmon, or lilac hues. Graphic landforms, glaciers that stretch for hundreds of miles, crevasses that could swallow entire skyscrapers, and strange ice and rock shapes seem wrought by a master sculptor. Because the air is extremely clear these features are visible from great distances and, without the contrast of vegetation or human presence, there is little sense of scale. Antarctica's coasts and wildlife are especially magnificent. Icebergs roam the high latitudes; rocky outcrops are home to penguins and seals.

Antarctica is of far greater value to the world than as just the last continent on which mankind has yet to make a significant impact. It is now regarded as the engine for much of the world's weather because of the powerful influence it has on southern air and seas. Samples taken from the depths of the Antarctic's ice cap are a chronicle of the earth's climate over thousands of years, yielding reference information about levels of carbon dioxide and other elements. As a monitoring site for keeping track of changes around the world, Antarctica is unsurpassed.

Should the wilderness values and scientific research opportunities of the Antarctic be threatened, the potential loss to humanity is enormous. During the last decade of this century the entire world, not just the Antarctic Treaty nations, must look closely to the future of the frozen continent. Hopefully, Antarctica will continue to be a venue for peaceful international scientific research and human fulfillment.

In six visits to Antarctica I have never ceased to be amazed by its wonders. From the windblown top of an unclimbed mountain to the icy-blue depths of a water-filled crevasse, the "last place on earth" has exerted its magnetic pull on me. As well as a sense of privilege for being lucky enough to have traveled there on so many occasions, one also feels a sense of responsibility. I have written this book to share the beauty and importance of the region with the many who may never be able to travel to the far south. Through these images and words I hope readers will gain a greater appreciation of the unique qualities of the Antarctic and why it should remain as it is—a pristine, untamed wilderness.

C H A P T E R   O N E

The White Continent:

The Geography of Antarctica

Antarctica's size and unique physical characteristics make this land of extremes so important to the world. Its weather, the seas that surround it, the pack ice, the ice cap itself, the mountains and glaciers, and the southern skies are all important and fascinating aspects of the Antarctic.

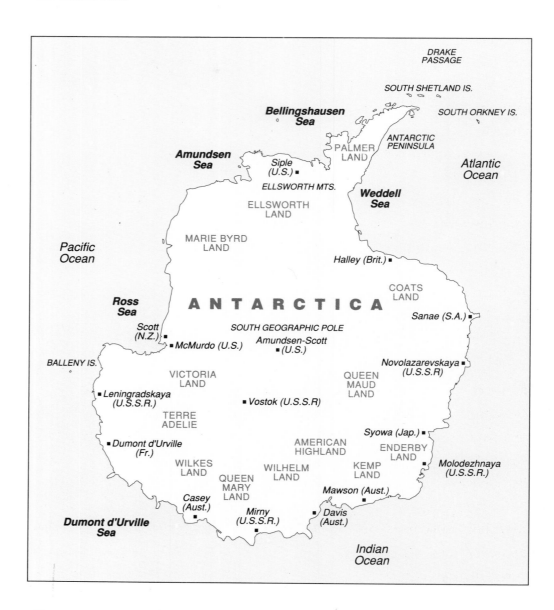

Antarctic Boundaries

What is regarded as the Antarctic varies with the seasons. The area covered by ice in the southern hemisphere more than doubles in the winter as the surface of the sea freezes. The sea ice reaches its maximum extent by September, but it continues to increase in thickness until October, when it can be over 5 feet (1.5 m) deep.

The increase in the area covered by the sea ice has enormous consequences for the climate, ecology, and isolation of continental Antarctica, as the discussions here and in chapters five and six on biology and shipping will show. Many maps of the region show both the average northern extent of pack ice (the winter maximum) and the average summer maximum. Antarctica is a movable place in more ways than just the expansion and contraction of the sea ice. The ice cap is also continually moving.

Those sailing to the Antarctic might feel that they have arrived once the first iceberg is sighted, or when they cross the Antarctic circle at 66°33S, or when they actually set foot on the continent itself. Scientists accept the biological limit of the Antarctic region (that is, the northern limit of creatures that make their homes in the far south) as the position of the Antarctic convergence—the zone where the colder southern waters sink between the warmer northern waters. This boundary varies from 60°S in the vicinity of South America to 50°S in the Indian Ocean, and also from season to season. The variations result from changes in winds, currents, and oceanographic conditions.

Those countries active on the continent or who cooperate in its management, known as the Antarctic Treaty nations, only concern themselves with the continent itself and ice cap south of 60°S. This definition excludes some islands and parts of the Southern Ocean that would ordinarily be regarded as Antarctica on the basis of their ecology.

But not all the political boundaries are so well defined. An international agreement that operates in conjunction with the Antarctic Treaty, the Convention for the Conservation of Antarctic Marine Living Resources (CCAMLR), tries to protect and manage the various species of the southern region on an ecosystem basis. CCAMLR uses the Antarctic convergence to delineate its sphere of interest. Thus it is clear that definitions of the far south vary to suit the needs of the interested parties.

Weather and Climate

Many people wonder why Antarctica is so cold and mostly covered in ice. Like the northern polar regions, Antarctica experiences dramatic seasonal changes that result from the earth's 23.5° tilt from the vertical axis. This means that for many weeks during midsummer (November to February) it is light twenty-four hours a day. In midwinter (June and July) there is a corresponding period of continual darkness when the sun never rises.

Overall, neither pole receives very much direct radiation from the sun, but the Antarctic is much colder than the Arctic for a variety of reasons. One is that there is about eight times more ice in the Antarctic than in the Arctic. This is because the Arctic is primarily an ocean, and water is better than land at storing the summer heat and moderating the winter cold. A second reason is that with Antarctica's year-round snow cover, nearly 80 percent of the incoming shortwave radiation is reflected back into the atmosphere. The sea, by comparison, reflects only 5 percent, while exposed land returns 15 to 35 percent.

Temperatures decrease with altitude as well as latitude. Much of the continent has a very high average altitude of 7,500 feet (2,286 m), which is an additional reason for it being so cold. The lowest temperature ever recorded on earth was at the Russian Antarctic station at Vostok in July 1983, when the thermometer recorded –128.6°F (89.2°C below freezing point). At this temperature steel shatters and water explodes into ice crystals. At the South Pole, winter temperatures average around –70°F (–56.6°C). Except for the Antarctic Peninsula, which extends much fur-

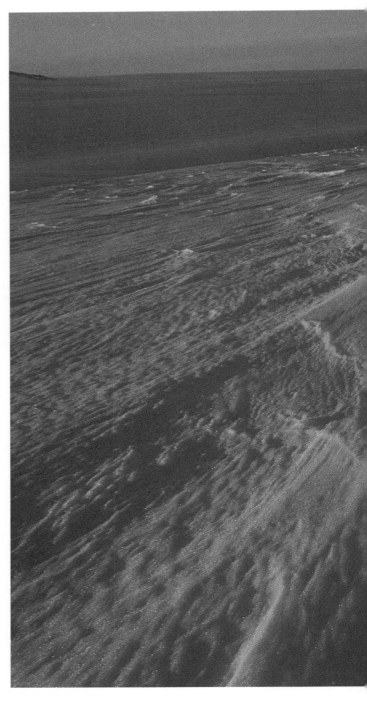

At Commonwealth Bay, the place Australian explorer Sir Douglas Mawson named "The Home of the Blizzard," katabatic winds regularly blast down off the ice cap at over 100 knots.

ther north than the rest of the continent, there is no part of the Antarctic that has a mean temperature above 32°F (0°C) in any month of the year.

Although Antarctica has more fresh water than any other continent, it also receives the least precipitation. The mean annual equivalent of only 2 inches (6 cm) of rainfall, lower than the precipitation in many desert areas, descends each year as snow or ice crystals. When it is snowing and windy at the same time in Antarctica, then the most ferocious conditions—blizzards—prevail. A severe blizzard may last for a week with visibility reduced to a few feet and winds blasting at up to 100 knots. While blizzards may carry freshly fallen snow, they are more frequently composed of drift snow that is picked up by the violent winds. Blizzards, which occur up to ten times a year in coastal areas, often cause severe damage to buildings and can bury structures under drift snow. Wind-packed drift snow will form fields of small, hard ridges known as sastrugi, which resemble frozen waves.

The Antarctic is also the windiest continent on earth. Very strong winds can blow throughout the year, sometimes reaching speeds of 200 miles per hour (320 kmph). These high winds combined with low temperatures make Antarctica an inhospitable place for humans. Antarctica's coastal areas are often the windiest because of the cold, dense air that flows down off the ice cap under the influence of gravity. These extremely regular and very strong winds are known as katabatic winds (*katabasis* is Greek for "descent"), and their speed and direction is controlled by the shape of the ice cap (the steeper the slope, the faster the wind). The most famous site for katabatic winds is Cape Denison at Commonwealth Bay, where Sir Douglas Mawson's Australasian Antarctic Expedition recorded the annual mean wind-speed average as 44 miles per hour (70 kmph)—the greatest wind speed at sea level on earth. Mawson wrote, "The climate proved little more than one continuous blizzard the year round; a hurricane of wind roaring for weeks

Much of the surface of the ice cap is sculpted into small ridges by these winds, called sastrugi. These undulations make surface travel very slow and uncomfortable.

Like all the species native to Antarctica, emperor penguins are well adapted to the rigors of the climate. In winter, they often walk for miles across the sea ice to open water to feed.

together, pausing for breath only at odd hours." It was little wonder he named this place "The Home of the Blizzard," which was also the name of the book he wrote about the expedition.

Antarctic weather can dramatically change in the space of a few hours. At its most benign, the temperature hovers around zero (perhaps even a few degrees higher if you are on the coast), and with no wind it may seem warm enough for people to strip off their clothes and sunbathe. Under these conditions visibility is usually excellent, since there is no haze or pollution; but the glare from the sun and the reflection from snow and ice can quickly result in snowblindness unless dark glasses are continuously worn.

The air in Antarctica is extremely dry. The low temperatures result in a very low absolute humidity (the amount of water vapor contained in a given volume of air), which means that dry skin and cracked lips are a continual problem for scientists and researchers working in the field. Large quantities of water vapor are lost from the lungs as well, making it necessary to frequently drink to replace the lost fluid. The low absolute humidity also dries out building timber very rapidly, contributing to a very high fire risk at Antarctica research stations.

Around the coast windy and clouded conditions often prevail. Low clouds and snow usually lead to a condition known as a "whiteout," during which no visual points of reference exist. Navigation under these conditions is exceedingly difficult and a compass is essential. If surface vehicles are operated regularly in places prone to whiteouts and blizzards, the regular routes will be marked by fuel drums or metal-tagged canes that can be picked up by radar. It is very easy to become disoriented in a whiteout, so flying becomes impossible and at sea, navigation also becomes difficult. The Air New Zealand DC-10 plane that crashed into Mount Erebus in 1979 was the result of navigational errors and a whiteout.

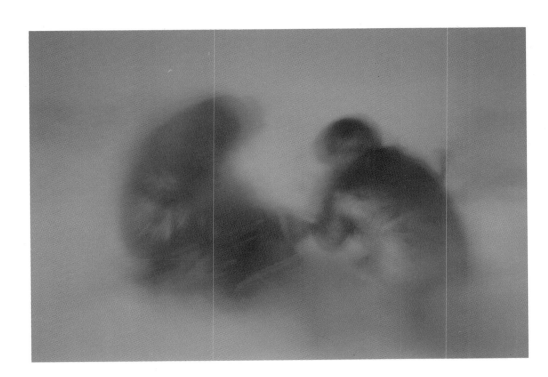

For humans, performing even simple tasks in an Antarctic blizzard can be a struggle. At times, the wind will bowl you over, and drifting snow can make it almost impossible to see.

The Seas Around Antarctica

The Antarctic is encircled by the Southern Ocean, which flows in a mostly eastward direction. This global movement, known as the Circumpolar Current, is driven by the strong westerly winds that circle the world in the high latitudes.

These powerful winds and depressions create some of the most tempestuous seas in the world. The high latitudes are appropriately known to sailors as the "roaring forties," "furious fifties," and "screaming sixties," and it is rare not to encounter at least one storm of mountainous proportions when sailing to and from the continent.

Immediately adjacent to the Antarctic is a countercirculation known as the Eastwind Drift. It is shallower and much less powerful than the Circumpolar Current, moving pack ice under its influence in a westerly direction.

The Southern Ocean is far from uniform with regard to sea temperatures. To the north, the zone where this ocean meets the warmer southflowing waters of the Atlantic, Pacific, and Indian oceans is known as the Antarctic Polar Front, or the convergence. The total area of sea within the convergence makes up one-tenth of all the world's oceans and contains the coolest and densest water to be found anywhere. A portion of this, known as Antarctic Bottom Water, which is rich in oxygen, spreads out over the world's ocean floors and causes the temperatures of much of the deep ocean to be cooled to less than 36°F (2°C). The cold affects much of the earth's climate by counterbalancing the heating effect of the tropics. Within the boundaries of the Southern Ocean, east-flowing water has a complex vertical circulation that draws water rich in nutrients to the surface. These nutrients are the basis for the highly productive nature of the southern seas. As well as being rich in marine life, the Southern Ocean plays a complex role in the heat exchange and formation of weather patterns with the continent.

Approaching the Antarctic by ship can be a long and arduous journey. The successive latitudes of the wild Southern Ocean are known as "the roaring forties," "furious fifties," and "screaming sixties" *(right)*. It is a chilly job keeping watch for floating ice and icebergs on the bow of a yacht on the final approach to the continent *(above)*.

Icebergs

Approaching Antarctica by sea is an exhilarating experience. Long before the continent can be seen, vestiges of its glaciers and ice shelves in the form of massive icebergs loom on the horizon. The icebergs, huge frozen masses of fresh water, are formed when parts of glaciers that push out into the sea or ice shelves (parts of the ice cap that have begun to float) break off and drift away. The separation is often a cataclysmic event, creating a boiling sea in the vicinity and a small tidal wave.

The Antarctic ice cap, which moves slowly but constantly, flows under its own massive weight toward the coast. In places, the ice protrudes into the surrounding waters. The effect of waves, swells, currents, and tides soon bend and twist the floating ice tongues and shelves, causing chunks of all sizes to break off; this is known as "calving." While the resulting icebergs do eventually melt, many last for years and even decades if they become grounded.

Icebergs form from giant chunks of ice cap that have broken off from the countless glaciers and ice shelves that jut out into the ocean. *Following page:* Towering ice cliffs surround much of Antarctica. For most of the year the sea lapping at the base of these cliffs is also covered by a layer of ice.

Icebergs have become symbols of Antarctica and are one of the most powerful images of the southern region. Icebergs have also been featured in literature. Edgar Allen Poe wrote in *The Narrative of A. Gordon Pym,* of "ramparts of ice…like the walls of the universe." There were also innumerable descriptions of icebergs in the journals of the early sealers and sailors.

Icebergs come in all shapes and sizes. As they melt and break up, the small pieces that they shed are given distinctive names such as "growlers," "bergy bits," and "brash," depending on their size. Icebergs themselves can also be categorized into tabular, irregular, or rounded icebergs, and their shape is usually an indication of their age. As a rule, Antarctica has much larger icebergs than the Arctic. A large Antarctic iceberg may weigh 400 million tons (363 million metric tons), tower ten stories above the surface of the water, and contain enough fresh water to supply a city of three million people for a year.

Each year an enormous number of icebergs calve from Antarctica, the total making up approximately 350 cubic miles (1,450 cubic km) of ice. Some icebergs that break off from the Antarctic shelf may measure as much as 1,000 square miles (2,600 sq km) in area and more than 900 feet (274 m) in depth. In 1963 one monster iceberg measuring 70 by 47 miles (112 by 75 km) was observed by satellite. This enormous iceberg lasted until 1970. One of the longest icebergs ever recorded, designated "B9," broke away from the Ross Ice Shelf in October 1987. The size of the state of Delaware, when it first calved it was measured at 86 by 22 nautical

miles (160 by 40 km). Since then, it has been drifting slowly at the speed of about 1 mile (1.6 km) per day in the Ross Sea. The largest icebergs originate from the ice shelves. The Ross Ice Shelf, a vast table of floating ice with a size as large as France, is gradually being pushed away from the Antarctic landmass.

Most icebergs are less than 180 yards (164 m) across at the waterline. The biggest icebergs, however, which account for only 4 percent by number, are 51 percent of the entire volume of ice. These giants are tabular icebergs, which calve from ice sheets and are often 650 to 1,000 feet (198 to 305 m) thick. The paths of icebergs larger than 6 miles (10 km) across can be plotted by satellite images. Icebergs mainly drift under the influence of currents, and their draft (the portion below the waterline) may cause them to run aground. Icebergs that drift northward melt faster in the warmer seas, but close to the Antarctic coast where the seawater temperature measures only 34°F (1°C), they can last for years. While melting does not play a big role in the disintegration of the larger icebergs, it is the main reason small icebergs eventually disappear. The amazing shapes that irregular and rounded icebergs often acquire is the result of melting underwater; when the icebergs roll upside down the sculpted forms become visible. This rotation takes place gradually at first, then when the iceberg becomes top-heavy and unstable it will turn over in a matter of seconds, often breaking into smaller pieces in the process. Such an event can be very dramatic, creating waves and a roar that can be heard for miles.

A tabular iceberg recently calved from the ice cap glows in the midnight sun off Cape Hallet, North Victoria Land.

Icebergs gradually become eroded by wind and waves and often take on unusual shapes and angles. Well-defined ridges are usually old water-lines *(top)*. If icebergs are grounded close to the continent they are usually set into fast ice in the winter *(bottom)*.

Upturned and rounded icebergs can be very smooth and often display a visible notch indicating the old waterline, where waves used to wash against it and erode it. Sometimes weird shapes, towers, or tunnels are formed by wave action beneath the surface. Some icebergs have bands or strips of jade-colored ice. Samuel Taylor Coleridge, in the lines of his poem "The Rime of the Ancient Mariner," immortalized these unique Antarctica sights:

> *And now there came both mist and snow,*
> *And it grew wondrous cold;*
> *And ice, mast-high,*
> *Came floating by,*
> *As green as emerald.*

Typically, icebergs do not survive at latitudes lower than the northern limit of Antarctic sea ice, near 48°S. Towing icebergs to dry southern Australian cities such as Perth and Adelaide has been proposed as a way of relieving these cities' fresh-water shortages during the summer. It is believed, however, that such a journey would take many months, in which time half the iceberg would have melted. The means by which the resulting fresh water could be harvested also presents a problem, because the icebergs have such a deep draft that they could not be towed

closer than about 20 miles (32 km) to the coast. Environmentalists also have expressed concern about the possible effects that melting icebergs could have on the local climates.

Pack Ice

While icebergs are the most visually exciting floating ice form, pack ice is more significant. In winter the sea around the Antarctic freezes, but ocean swells and wind break sea ice, as it is known, into larger pieces (pack ice) that move under the influence of wind and currents. "Fast ice" is sea ice that is held fast to the continent. The extent and nature of the sea ice plays a vital role in the earth's weather system. While open ocean reflects only 5 percent of incoming solar radiation, snow-covered pack ice reflects more than 80 percent. Pack ice reaches its maximum extent in September and October when the sun's radiation over the southern hemisphere is increasing. The pack ice helps to keep the Antarctic cold by delaying the warming effects of the sun.

Sea ice buildup is the most extensive seasonal process in the world's oceans and it more than quadruples the area of Antarctica, from approximately 1 million square miles (3.8 million sq km) to 7.7 million square miles (20 million sq km). The area covered by ice during this seasonal change is greater than the whole area of the Antarctic continent itself.

Small and medium pieces of floating sea ice are called brash ice or bergy bits.

Open pack ice occurs each summer around the continent as the fast ice breaks up under the influence of higher temperatures, wind, and waves.

There are distinct stages in the transition from seawater to sea ice. Because of its salt content, seawater usually begins to freeze at −28°F (−1.8°C). First, crystals form on the surface of the brine, creating an oily sheen known as grease ice. This further evolves into a slush known as frazil ice. The sea ice gradually thickens as more and more water from below freezes and as snow falls from above. The next stage is nilas, which is a thin elastic crust of ice up to 4 inches (10 cm) thick that bends easily when influenced by swells and waves. Ocean swells and waves may cause the grease ice to break apart and refreeze several times before forming a solid sheet. In this process disks of ice with turned-up edges result from being bumped together, forming pancake ice. While sea ice is extensive around the continent, it by no means forms a continuous mass even at its peak. It is broken up by large shifting areas of open water, known as polynyas. These may measure up to 60 miles (96 km) across.

The sea ice tends to grow quickly at first, reaching half its maximum thickness within a month. The freezing-over of the sea usually begins in late March (autumn). The breakup of the sea ice in spring (October to January) happens even faster, possibly due to the presence of pigmented algae, which, being darker than ice, absorbs more solar radiation. Sometimes the sea ice builds up over successive seasons, and, as this occurs, the salt is gradually leached from the ice into the surrounding ocean to the point where the water from melted sea ice is quite drinkable. Melted water from old sea ice and icebergs was the main way that early Antarctica-bound ships were able to replenish their water supplies.

Our knowledge of sea ice today has been increased enormously due to
the information relayed by polar-orbiting satellites. This information
can be translated into charts showing pack ice distribution, a boon to
researchers and navigators. The thickness and extent of pack ice and
fast ice are the main reasons that ships, even ice-strengthened vessels,
cannot reach Antarctic research stations for much of the year. Most ship-
based scientific research cruises are also limited to the summer months,
which is why we know so little about the science of sea ice. Pack ice
moves mostly under the influence of the wind and surface currents.
It can change in a matter of hours from being densely packed and
impassable to non-icebreaking vessels to "open pack," as it is known.
Wide gaps in pack ice are known as leads, which are sought by ship's
captains trying to navigate close to the continent.

Until the fast ice breaks up,
ships are unable to reach the continent
proper.

The Ice Cap

The Antarctic continent is vast. It covers about 5.4 million square miles (40 million sq km), about one-and-a-half times the size of the United States. Antarctica is also the highest continent in the world, with an estimated average altitude of 7,500 feet (2,300 m). In comparison, the next highest continent, Asia, has an average height of only about 2,900 feet (884 m), in spite of the presence of Mount Everest and the mighty Himalaya. Australia's average altitude is only 1,100 feet (335 m). Virtually the entire Antarctic continent is covered by ice with an average thickness of .93 miles (1.5 km). The weight of the Antarctic ice is so great that in many areas it actually pushes the land below sea level. This process of the earth's crust being deformed is known as isostasy. Without the ice cover Antarctica would eventually rise about 1,500 feet (457 m) above sea level.

The Antarctic ice cap contains almost 7.2 million cubic miles (30 million cubic km) of ice — about 90 percent of all ice existing in the world and 68 percent of the world's fresh water. This ice has built up over 100,000 years of compacted snowfall. All the ice on the continent is very gradually moving toward the sea in a radial pattern. For example, a snowflake falling at the South Pole would take up to 50,000 years to reach the ocean. Most of the snowfall occurs along the coast.

From the air, the scale of towering ice cliffs, giant melt lakes, and rivers of ice on the edge of the continent is difficult to gauge.

The balancing of accumulated snow with the loss of ice by ablation (where the ice turns directly into water vapor), melting, and calving icebergs is of great interest to glaciologists. Currently, the Antarctic ice cap is believed to be in equilibrium, but if all the ice on the continent melted it would raise the levels of the world's oceans by 200 to 210 feet (61 to 64 m), thus submerging many coastal cities. The possibility of this happening in the short term is not seriously considered by scientists. Meteorologists studying the ramifications of global warming and the greenhouse effect expect there to be a decrease in sea levels in the short term (decades) of about .12 inches (3 mm) per year. This will be due to an increase in the amount of water vapor in the air as a result of higher air temperatures, and will lead to greater snowfall on the continent. Over the longer term, higher global air temperatures are expected to generate higher ice cap flow rates and more icebergs, which are expected to lead to a rise in sea levels of 2 feet (.6 m) after 100 years.

While most of Antarctica is covered by an ice cap, within this system there are distinct glaciers, the majority of which occur on the coast. The largest in the world is the Lambert Glacier, in the vicinity of the Prince Charles Mountains. Some 25 miles (40 km) wide and 250 miles (400 km) long, the Lambert Glacier drains a vast area. The most famous Antarctic glacier, however, is the Beardmore, which served as a pathway for early explorers such as Robert F. Scott and Ernest Shackleton on their way to the South Pole.

Icefall *(top)* and ice cliffs *(above)* in the Antarctic are less active than in other parts of the world because of the intense cold.

Mountains and Oases

Only between 2 and 4 percent of the Antarctic is snow-free. The main areas without snow are the isolated tips of mountains (nunataks) and the edges of the continent where the ice sheet leaves exposed rocks and oases.

The Vestfold Hills is one of the larger oases in Antarctica *(top)*. This region and the nearby Rauer Islands *(bottom)* in Prydz Bay are examples of the types of areas that make up the 4 percent of Antarctica that is permanently snow free.

Oases are large areas of snow-free land that look more akin to the deserts of lower latitudes. They only occur in East Antarctica, and the largest of these are the dry valleys of Victoria Land on the edge of the Ross Sea. The three main valleys, the Taylor, the Wright, and the Victoria, were once filled with glaciers that have long since retreated. Once oases lose their glacial ice, their conditions become self-perpetuating, because the dark, exposed surface absorbs sufficient heat to melt winter snows, while the strong winds help to blow any drift snow away. The floors of the dry valleys are strewn with oddly shaped rocks known as ventifacts, which are eroded by sandblasting winds. It is suggested that no rain has fallen in these dry valleys for the last two million years.

Other significant oases in Antarctica are the Bunger Hills, the Vestfold Hills, the Prince Charles Mountains, and the Lasserman Hills. Oases often contain both fresh and saline lakes fed by streams that flow for a few weeks during the summer from glacier tongues. Such lakes occasionally contain aquatic life.

Mountain ranges that rise above the ice cap are other significant snow-free sites. The Antarctic has one of the longest mountain chains in the world—the Transantarctic Mountains—that extend from the tip of the Antarctic Peninsula to Cape Adare, a distance of 3,000 miles (4,800 km). In many places the chain is buried, but in the areas where the peaks are exposed, they often have steep, snow-free faces.

There are numerous other mountain ranges in the Antarctic, including the Prince Charles Mountains, the Shackleton Range, the Ford Range, and the Pensacola Mountains. There are also countless exposed islands of rock or nunataks that appear just above the ice.

The tallest mountain in Antarctica is the Vinson Massif in the Sentinel Range, towering 16,864 feet (5,140 m) above sea level. Named after an American chairman of the House Armed Services Committee, Carl Vinson, the peak was established as the highest by an American traverse party in 1957. The Sentinel Range was first discovered by Lincoln Ellsworth in 1935 on his epic transcontinental flight, and is considered part of a larger area of mountains that now bears his name. Vinson Massif was first climbed in December 1966 by an American expedition. In summer the peak is a popular destination for mountaineers who attempt to climb the highest point on all seven continents. During the summer a private Canadian airline operates a charter service into the Ellsworth Mountains for tourists and climbers.

Around the edges of East Antarctica are numerous, smaller, snow-free areas and islands where the bare rock occurs as a result of the effects of local topography and contortions of the ice cap. The main wildlife breeding colonies can be found here and are also the most popular sites for permanent scientific stations.

The slopes of Admiralty Mountain in North Victoria Land illustrate the rugged nature of much of the Trans Antarctic Mountains.

Southern Skies

Antarctic skies are extremely clear. With little free moisture and no dust, there is almost no haze. Southern skies do, however, feature a number of unique visual phenomena: auroras, parhelia, sun dogs or mock suns, sun pillars, and mirages. Parhelia and sun dogs or mock suns are halos that form around the sun or moon in the shape of circles, arcs, or spots. They appear to the observer when light is scattered, diffracted, reflected, or refracted off ice crystals that occur in clouds or are just suspended in the air. Sun pillars, vertical shafts of glowing rays, are also the result of ice crystals in the sky at sunset. Such effects were made famous by Edward Wilson, a member of Robert Falcon Scott's 1901 expedition, in his water-colors, particularly *Paraselena. Cape Evans. McMurdo Sound.*

Catching the late evening sun in summer on the pack ice is one of the most photogenic times in the Antarctic.

Possibly the most spectacular of the visual phenomena in the southern skies are the auroras. Auroras can only be seen when the sky is dark, so most summer visitors to the continent miss seeing them. The aurora australis or "southern dawn" (the southern hemisphere's version of the northern aurora borealis) is a form of electrical disturbance 50 to 595 miles (80 to 952 km) up in the stratosphere. Auroral displays appear in the night sky as beautiful colored arcs, bands, and even waving-curtain effects of light. These can shimmer and pulse in displays that last for minutes or hours. Auroras in the southern hemisphere are concentrated in an oval shape about 30° north of the magnetic axis of the earth—the South Magnetic Pole. They are extremely difficult to photograph because they are very faint and can move rapidly and change color.

The final main visual phenomena in the Antarctic, mirages, are more commonly found in hot deserts, but they also occur at the poles. Here they are caused by low-slanting sunlight that passes through layers of cold air close to the surface refracting toward the observer. These are known as superior mirages, causing objects to appear to float in the shimmering air and seem closer than they really are.

There can be little doubt that the Antarctic is a fascinating place for scientists today, but there is an equally interesting story there for paleontologists, geologists, and those interested in the origins of the continent and how it came to be over the South Pole.

Summer or winter, spectacular visual phenomena are often to be seen in Antarctic skies. When darkness comes to the night sky, the colorful aurora australis, or southern lights *(top left)*, is regularly seen in the auroral belt, thirty degrees north of the south magnetic pole. The reflection of light off snow crystals in the atmosphere are the cause of solar pillars *(top right)* and parhelia, rings around the sun *(bottom right)*. Shadows cast from the mountains at sunset can also have an unearthly feel *(bottom left)*.

The Origins of Antarctica:

Gondwanaland

People often ask why Antarctica is located where it is today and why it is so different from the rest of the world. The answers to these questions lie in the theories of continental drift, which explains the breakup of an ancient landmass, Gondwanaland, and the subsequent development of the ocean current that today encircles the southern continent.

The Antarctic ice cap now is similar to those that enveloped much of Europe and North America during the periods known as the Ice Ages. Examination of the Antarctic ice cap can shed light on the mechanism and processes of glaciation, the formation of ice sheets, and frost action that shaped the earth elsewhere, particularly in the northern hemisphere. Scientists believe that unraveling the complex set of factors that precipitate ice ages holds important clues about the geological and climatic changes in the world today.

Fossils discovered in such diverse places such as Marine Plain in the Vestfold Hills indicate that a very different environment and climate once was present in Antarctica.

Continental Drift

The Antarctic continent as we know it today has not always been located in the position it now occupies, nor has it always been so cold. The presence of coal (which is formed from ancient vegetation) and fossils of tropical plants and animals show that Antarctica was once considerably warmer. Scientists believe that this was long before the continent drifted to its present position over the South Pole.

The idea of continental drift was first proposed by Alfred Wegener in 1912, but it was another forty years before there was scientific evidence to support his ideas. Wegener suggested that the continents were not fixed in position but were constantly moving relative to one another. Plate tectonics, as the process of continental drift is known, is today a major area of study in its own right. Geologists now believe that the surface of the earth is made up of six solid plates that "float" on a core of magma (molten rock). This theory explains mid-ocean ridges, which form when two plates are moving apart, volcanoes, and earthquake zones, which occur when plates grate together. It is the theory of plate tectonics that has helped to explain the evolution of the Antarctic, not to mention the formation and position of every other continent on the globe.

As glaciers retreat, highly polished and scoured rock surfaces are regularly exposed in many places around the continent.

The Frammes Mountains in Mac Robertson Land are one of many smaller ranges around the perimeter of the Antarctic continent that geologists have studied.

Gondwanaland

Antarctica as it appears today has existed for only the past sixty million years. To picture the origins of the continent it is necessary to go back in time to the giant southern hemisphere landmass known as Gondwanaland, which existed from 500 million years ago to 160 million years ago. At this time the eastern part of Antarctica formed the core of the "super continent," which also included Africa, South America, India, Australia, and New Zealand. The evidence for this link can be found in the similar geology of the southern parts of these continents.

By sixty million years ago, the convection currents within the earth's magma had begun, through continental drift, to form a deep ocean between the Antarctic and Australia as the continents moved apart. What is now known as the Drake Passage, the sea route between Antarctica and South America, also began to open. This led to the formation of the Antarctic Circumpolar Current twenty-eight million years ago, which isolated the continent from the warmer oceans of the world and from severe climatic change. In response to this cooling, all the forests, ferns, freshwater fish, amphibians, and reptiles disappeared and the Antarctic became covered with ice. Today, evidence of this erstwhile flora and fauna only appears in the form of fossils.

The Antarctic is divided into two main regions, the east called East Antarctica or "Greater Antarctica," and the west known as West Antarctica or "Lesser Antarctica," both east and west are quite different geologically. Greater Antarctica consists of a stable shield of very ancient rocks (pre-Cambrian) older than 570 million years and mostly above sea level. Some rocks have been dated as far back as 380 million years. If the ice cap were removed, West Antarctica would simply be a string of islands. The two regions are separated by the Transantarctic Mountains, and in most places, peaks protrude above the ice cap. But the remainder of the topography of the continent is mainly hidden beneath the ice.

Ice Ages

The ice ages were those periods during the earth's history when large portions of the earth were covered by ice caps. There have been some ten ice ages during the last one million years, occurring at intervals of about 100,000 years. Geological records suggest that the ice ages developed slowly but disappeared relatively quickly. Their cause has long puzzled scientists.

Exposed fossils *(left)* and rock strata on the edge of the continent *(right)* are two of the main sources of information about the geological history of the terrain beneath the ice cap.

It is now believed that a cycle of the three main irregularities, or wobbles, in the earth's orbit are the main factors that initiate an ice age. These are firstly the variations in the tilt of the earth's axis from 22° to 25°, which occurs in a cycle that repeats itself every 41,000 years (a change in the tilt alters the amount of heat from the sun that reaches the polar regions). The second irregularity is the procession, movement along a path, which completes its cycle every 21,000 years. This determines the season at which the earth is closest to the sun during its orbit. Currently, the earth is further from the sun during the northern hemisphere's summer than it is during its winter. The third cycle, with a period of 100,000 years, alters the shape of the earth's orbit and amplifies or minimizes the effect of the procession. This theory was first proposed in the 1870s by an amateur Scottish scientist, James Croll, and was verified in the 1920s by a Serbian mathematician, Milutin Milankovitch. He showed that these variations were the basis for the significantly cooler summers every 21,000 and 41,000 years. Such changes may have helped to cause an ice age by beginning a buildup of ice at the poles. The additional time it took for the ice sheets to grow to their maximum sustainable size has been suggested as a reason for the ice ages falling every 100,000 years. There are, however, varying theories on the mechanisms that amplify the Milankovitch wobbles and cause the ice ages to develop faster and end more rapidly than the original theory would suggest.

Exposed sedimentary rock in the Rauer Islands shows how parts of the continent were once covered by the sea.

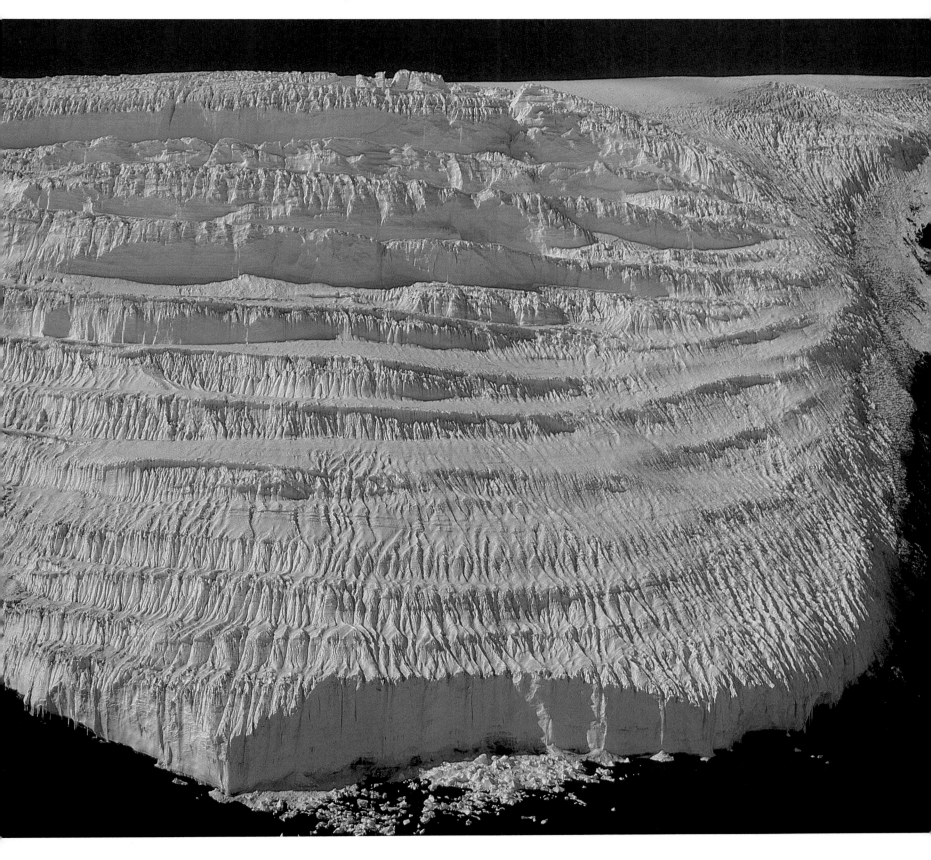

There is a suggestion among scientists that the world is heading into another ice age. Others believe that the opposite is occurring. In fact, for the first time in human history there is the possibility that the world's climatic cycle is being changed through a buildup of carbon dioxide, resulting in global warming. It has been suggested that the effects of global warming will first be visible in the ice-covered parts of the planet. We therefore need to have a much greater understanding of Antarctic geography, glaciology, and ecology in order to effectively monitor and predict such changes.

The giant hanging glaciers at Cape Hallet, many thousands of feet high, illustrate the scale of glaciation in Antarctica.

Sailors, Heroes, and Scientists:

The Exploration of Antarctica

The possibility of a giant continent in the southern hemisphere was first hypothesized by the Greeks. They named it *Terra Australis.*

The discovery and exploration of Antarctica is quite recent in terms of human history. All the discoveries have taken place in just 200 years. The major milestones were Captain James Cook's crossing of the Antarctic Circle in 1773, the first sighting of Antarctica by sailing ships in 1820, the first winter spent on the continent in 1898, and the race for the South Pole that began in 1904 and culminated in Amundsen's success in 1911. While the exploration of Antarctica can be divided into the Heroic Age, the Mechanical Age, and the Age of Science, in every phase there have been outstanding examples of human courage and the questing spirit.

Terra Australis

The Ancient Greeks were the first to suggest the existence of Antarctica. Deducing that the world was a sphere, they imagined there had to be a landmass to the south to balance Europe and Asia in the north. Otherwise, it was believed, the globe would topple over. They named this place, *Antarktikos,* which means "opposite the bear" (*arktos*), the constellation above the North Pole. The term *arktos* was modified to Arctic and was used to describe the north polar region. Antarctic is a shortening of Anti-Arctic, or opposite the Arctic. From the time of Columbus on, mapmakers almost always included a continent described as "Terra Australis Incognita" (the unknown Southern land) situated exactly where the Antarctic is now. According to Polynesian legends, the first human to encounter the Antarctic realm may well have been a seventh-century Raratongan traveler, Ui-te-Rangiara, who, it is said, "sailed south to a place of bitter cold where white rocklike forms grew out of a frozen sea."

There were numerous voyages into subantarctic waters by the sailors and explorers during the sixteenth and seventeenth centuries, many of whom were blown off course. The first recorded crossing of the Antarctic Circle, however, was in 1773 by the English captain James Cook and crews aboard the *Resolution* and the *Adventure*. Altogether Cook made three voyages through Antarctic waters. Though never actually sighting the continent, he was convinced there was a "tract of land at the Pole that is the source of all the ice that is spread over this vast Southern Ocean." Cook reached 71°S, farther south than anyone before him, and in three years sailed some 62,000 miles (99,200 km) in possibly the greatest sea voyage ever made.

Cook's voyages were followed by a period when American and British sealers traveled south, discovering subantarctic islands. From these islands they slaughtered fur seals for their skins and elephant seals for their oil. It was possibly a member of one of these sealing parties, Admiral Fabian von Bellingshausen, who made the first sighting of the Antarctic continent in January 1820. A British officer, Edward Bransfield, sighted the Antarctic Peninsula a month later, and Nathaniel Palmer, an American sealer, also claimed a sighting in November 1820.

Scientific expeditions followed in the wake of the sealing parties. From the late 1830s onward investigations into the earth's magnetic fields encouraged expeditions to set out to locate the South Magnetic Pole. The magnetic poles, one in each hemisphere, are the points where the earth's magnetic lines pass into the earth. At these points, the magnetic or dip poles, a compass needle will stand vertically. The North Magnetic Pole was discovered in 1831, sparking competition among scientific teams from several different countries to find the southern equivalent.

When James Cook became the first undisputed navigator to cross the Antarctic Circle in 1773, he encountered icebergs and pack ice, and was unable to proceed any further south.

A Frenchman, J. S. C. Dumont d'Urville, and an American, Charles Wilkes, searched for the South Magnetic Pole in 1840, but they were unsuccessful in their pursuit. The following year James Clark Ross of Great Britain sailed into what is now the Ross Sea and determined the approximate position of the South Magnetic Pole, but was unable to reach it. He was successful, however, in charting unknown territory. This included discovering a giant ice shelf the size of the state of Texas, and it was later named after him.

The Heroic Age

The first party to land on the continent beyond the Antarctic Peninsula was part of a whaling expedition aboard the *Antarctic.* Led by Norwegian Henrich Bull, they rowed ashore at Cape Adare in January 1895. A dispute later arose as to whether it had been Bull or another member of the party, Carsten Borchgrevink, who had been first to land.

The first great scientific expedition of this era began in 1897, led by a Belgian, Adrien de Gerlache. Among his ship's complement were Roald Amundsen, Dr. Frederick Cook, and Henry Arctowski, all of whom were to make names for themselves in polar exploration. Their ship, the *Belgica,* was beset by ice off the Antarctic Peninsula, and they spent thirteen months drifting in the pack ice. This expedition is credited with being the first to winter in Antarctica, albeit unintentionally. The privations of this enforced stay were severe; one of the crew died of a heart attack and two more were committed to an asylum on their return. They endured inadequate food supplies, little heating, and low morale on a vessel ill-equipped to face the Antarctic winter. Dr. Frederick Cook, a seasoned Arctic explorer, coped best and took unofficial command.

The first expedition to deliberately spend a winter on the continent were explorers from the vessel the *Southern Cross.* They established a base of prefabricated huts at Cape Adare, North Victoria Land, in 1899. The party was led by Carsten Borchgrevink, who had landed at the same place with Henrich Bull four years earlier. (One of their huts still survives and is a historic monument.)

The Race for the South Pole

At the turn of the century the race to reach the South Pole became the focus for explorers and rapidly caught the imagination of the European public.

When talking about the pole, a distinction must be made between the South Geographic Pole and the South Magnetic Pole. The Magnetic Pole, as explained earlier, is the southern point where the earth's magnetic lines pass into the ground. The Geographic Pole is the point around which the earth revolves. The South Magnetic Pole in fact moves about, and when first being sought was located in Victoria Land some 1,200 miles (1,920 km) from the South Geographic Pole.

In 1901, Robert Falcon Scott led a British naval expedition to the Ross Sea. After wintering at Hut Point on Ross Island, Scott and five men pushed inland to within 450 miles (720 km) of the South Geographic Pole, but finally turned back in despair.

At the end of the first winter, one of Scott's party, Ernest Shackleton, was sent home on the resupply ship, reputedly suffering from scurvy. His sense of honor tarnished, he decided to return at the head of his own expedition. In 1907, Shackleton led the British Antarctic Expedition (BAE) back to the Ross Sea. After wintering at Cape Royds on Ross Island, Shackleton and a team of three sledged to 97 miles (155 km) from the South Geographic Pole. Realizing his party had insufficient supplies to reach the pole and return safely, Shackleton opted to stop short of his goal rather than risk disaster. While Shackleton was engaged with the South Geographic Pole, other members of his expedition, including Australians Douglas Mawson and Tannatt Edgeworth David, and a Scottish doctor, Alistair McKay, also set out from the winter quarters on Ross Island. They became the first party to reach the South Magnetic Pole. Shackleton's expedition also made the first ascent of Mount Erebus, the 12,450 foot (3,795 m) active volcano on Ross Island.

Shackleton's Hut at Cape Royds on Ross Island has been maintained as a historic monument by New Zealanders since 1959.

In 1911 Scott returned to Antarctica for a second attempt at the elusive South Geographic Pole. Further to the east—and unbeknownst to Scott—a Norwegian party was also wintering with its sights firmly fixed on reaching the pole first. Its leader, Roald Amundsen, was a dedicated explorer with considerable polar experience, having been on de Gerlache's historic expedition in 1897. His team had several factors in their favor. Their base at the Bay of Whales was 69 miles (110 km) closer to the pole than Scott's on Ross Island. The Norwegians set out thirteen days before Scott and had the added advantage of fifty-nine husky dogs hauling their sleds and the skill to use them to maximum advantage. Scott had opted to use ponies and dogs but the ponies weren't able to

Above: The interior of Shackleton's Hut has been restored to a state similar to how it had been left in 1909 by the British Antarctic Expedition, who had sledged to within ninety-seven miles (155 km) of the South Pole. *Opposite page:* The early exploration of much of Antarctica was mostly done on foot or by dog team. For parties on the ground today the conditions are unchanged.

haul in soft snow and the dogs were used only as support. Scott's party was soon reduced to hauling their supplies themselves. In short, Amundsen's party was better managed and able to move more swiftly.

On December 14, 1911, after fifty-seven days on the move, Amundsen, four companions, and eighteen dogs (out of a total of fifty-nine) finally reached the South Geographic Pole. They had pioneered a new route onto the polar plateau. Amundsen's party returned to the Bay of Whales without mishap and set sail to Australia to inform the world of their triumph.

The second group, consisting of Robert Scott, Bill Wilson, Henry "Birdie" Bowers, Edward Edgar Evans, and Lawrence "Titus" Oates, finally reached the pole a month later, only to find the tent Amundsen had left behind flying the Norwegian flag. Inside, Scott found letters for the King of Norway. Scott noted in his diary: "This is an awful place and terrible enough for us to have labored to without the reward of priority." Scott and his team, bitter with disappointment and debilitated by frostbite, set off for their base on the coast. On the way back, in a courageous act of self-sacrifice, Titus Oates, realizing his weak condition was slowing down the party, walked out of the tent and was never seen again. The rest of the party struggled on, but was eventually pinned down for eight days by bad weather, ironically just 11 miles (18 km) from their "one ton" supply depot. They all perished. Their fate was not discovered until the next summer when a search party dug out their almost completely buried camp. It was a tragic sight. Among their possessions were 35 pounds (16 kg) of rock samples — a testimony either to their dedication to science or their foolhardiness.

Countless other stories of extreme hardship and privation in the name of science and exploration emerged throughout these early years of Antarctic exploration. Many nationalities were involved. Australia's Douglas. Mawson was the driving force and leader of the 1911–14 Australasian Antarctic Expedition (AAE). The team spent two winters at Commonwealth Bay, the windiest place in the world, the place Mawson later made famous in his book *The Home of the Blizzard*. It was on his first expedition with Shackleton on the sledging journey to the South Magnetic Pole that Mawson conceived the idea of organizing his own expedition to explore the area of Antarctica due south of Australia, about which very little was known. The Australasian Antarctic Expedition is today regarded as one of the greatest polar scientific expeditions of all time, because of the detailed observations made in magnetism, geology, biology, and meteorology. More than anything else, it was Mawson's personal struggle against almost overwhelming odds during the course of the AAE that secured him a place in history. He overcame starvation, poisoning, blizzards, and innumerable falls into gaping crevasses as he struggled back, alone, to the winter quarters at Cape Denison following the deaths of his sledging companions, Xavier Mertz and Belgrade Ninnis.

Douglas Mawson *(above)* was only twenty-nine when he organized the Australasian Antarctic Expedition (AAE). This expedition made the first ever radio transmission from the Antarctic to the outside world *(right)* from the workshop adjoining the main hut at Cape Denison *(opposite page, bottom)*. On a spring sledging journey, Mawson's companion, Ninnis, was lost down one of the hidden giant crevasses that abound on the ice cap *(opposite page, top)*. Mertz also died, leaving Mawson to struggle back to base alone, with little food or shelter.

While on a sledging expedition to the east of the main base Ninnis, six dogs, and the sled containing most of the party's food and equipment were lost down a bottomless crevasse. Mawson and Mertz began an epic trek back to their base. With little food and only a makeshift tent, they were forced to kill and eat the remaining emaciated huskies to survive. One hundred miles (160 km) from Cape Denison, Mertz became delirious and eventually died. Mawson was also very ill from what was later diagnosed as vitamin A poisoning, contracted from eating the dogs' livers. He finally struggled back to Cape Denison to see the relief ship, the

Previous page: Today, Mawson's
**Hut still stands at Cape Denison, Common-
wealth Bay, despite having been battered by
blizzards for nearly eighty years. The interior is almost wholly filled with snow and ice.
Mawson's cubicle with his chair and bed still
survive, but in a dilapidated condition.
Above: Books and magazines found in the
interior of Mawson's Hut provide an idea of
how the early explorers spent their time during the long winter darkness.**

Aurora, disappearing over the horizon. Mawson and six others endured
a second winter at the windiest place in the world before finally being
rescued the following season.

Although the South Geographic Pole had finally been won, there were
still great challenges to be overcome and a great deal that remained
to be discovered.

On the eve of the First World War, Shackleton returned to the Antarctic. His goal on this occasion was to traverse the entire continent with
an expedition that consisted of two teams. The support party traveled
to Ross Island aboard the *Aurora,* the same vessel that had carried
Mawson's Australasian Antarctic Expedition to Commonwealth Bay in
1911. Its task was to establish supply depots on the route to the South
Pole for the main party approaching the continent via the Weddell Sea.

In 1915, Shackleton's main party was still aboard their ship, the
Endurance, when it became frozen in the sea ice long before they could
reach their intended landing point. The ship was forced to become their
winter quarters, but gradually the pressure of the ice began to crush the
vessel. Eventually all twenty-eight men pitched tents on the ice and
watched as the *Endurance* broke up and disappeared beneath the pack
ice. In 281 days they drifted 15,000 miles (24,000 km), but were still 350
miles (560 km) from the coast. After several attempts to walk and haul
their lifeboats toward open water, they eventually made camp and
waited until the pack ice broke up. The entire complement then set sail

to Elephant Island. There, under the leadership of Shackleton's devoted second-in-command, Frank Wild, most of the party spent the remainder of the bitter winter living under upturned boats and eating seal meat. Soon after arriving, Shackleton and a crew of five set out on one of the most astonishing small boat journeys of all time. Buffeted by mountainous waves they navigated 800 miles (1,280 km) in the 18-foot (5-m) *James Caird* to South Georgia. Landing on the wrong side of the island, they crossed the mountainous spine with virtually no supplies or climbing equipment, eventually reaching the Stromness whaling station. Shackleton then immediately set off in a Norwegian whaler to rescue the rest of the party from Elephant Island, but pack ice prevented them from reaching their goal. On a third attempt in the Chilean steamer *Yelcho* the whole team was eventually rescued. Not a single life was lost during the entire expedition.

The pioneers of the Antarctic had to contend with many dangers in their explorations. Their ships were often beset in the pack ice, and once on the ice cap they risked being swallowed by a crevasse or falling over giant ice cliffs.

The Ross Sea support party fared much worse. Their ship was blown away from its winter moorings and the shore party was left with almost no supplies, save what remained in the hut from the previous expeditions. The following spring those left ashore still managed to lay out resupply depots of the rations they had pieced together, unaware of the fate of the *Endurance* party on the other side of the continent.

In the process of returning to their winter quarters one of the Ross Sea support party died of scurvy. Later, two more attempted to beat a path back to Cape Evans across newly formed sea ice and were never seen again. The rest of the party was eventually rescued by the *Aurora* in January 1917.

The saga of Shackleton's failed Trans-Antarctic Expedition has become a classic tale of leadership and heroism, more famous even perhaps than Amundsen's achievement in reaching the South Pole.

In 1921 Shackleton was drawn back once more to the Antarctic to attempt to map 2,000 miles (3,200 km) of coastline and conduct meteorological and geological research. Although he was only forty-eight, he died of a suspected heart attack on board the *Quest*. Shackleton was buried in South Georgia and his death brought to a close the "Heroic" or so-called "Golden Era" of Antarctic exploration.

Amundsen and Mawson both used huskies to their considerable advantage on sledging journeys in Antarctica.

The Mechanical Age

World War I slowed polar exploration for a time. Only the British maintained any form of scientific research. Using Scott's old ship, the *Discovery,* they made thirteen successive summer cruises in the Southern Ocean to investigate the biology and oceanography of the region.

During the 1920s and 1930s the increasing use of planes, tractors, and motorized toboggans was soon to herald a new era in exploration. Australian-born Herbert Wilkins introduced the airplane and aerial photography to Antarctica in 1928, making a flight from Deception Island across the Antarctic Peninsula in a Lockheed Vega monoplane. He successfully traversed most of the length of Graham Land, but incorrectly concluded that it was divided into four islands.

The British, Australian, and New Zealand Antarctic Research Expedition (BANZARE), under the leadership of the Antarctic veteran Sir Douglas Mawson, set off from Cape Town in 1929. Over the next two summer seasons the BANZARE discovered Mac Robertson Land and charted long sections of Antarctic coastline. A float plane was also used for reconnaissance on this expedition.

It was United States Admiral Richard E. Byrd who became the first person to fly over the South Pole on the first of his five expeditions to Antarctica. In 1929 he and three others made a ten-hour flight in a Ford monoplane from his Little America base on the Ross Ice Shelf.

Another American, Lincoln Ellsworth, was the next significant pioneer to use aviation as a means of exploring the Antarctic. In 1935, on his third attempt, he and pilot Herbert Hollick-Kenyon made the first successful flight across the Antarctic. The journey was made in four stages and began from Dundee Island, but their plane ran out of fuel just 16 miles (26 km) short of Byrd's old base at the Bay of Whales. On this and later expeditions in the 1930s, Ellsworth claimed 300,000 square miles (777,000 sq km) of the Antarctic for his country, but the United States government did not follow up on this and other similar claims, and nothing came of them.

Antarctica had long been a bastion of male explorers, but in 1935 the wife of a Norwegian whaling captain became the first woman to land on the continent when she stepped ashore in the Vestfold Hills. The first women to winter in Antarctica were Edith Ronnie and Jennie Darlington, who, in 1947–48, accompanied their husbands on a private American expedition that made a base on Stonington Island on the Antarctic Peninsula.

In 1940, Admiral Byrd returned to the continent. He established his Little America III Base at the Bay of Whales and organized extensive exploration of the Marie Byrd Land coast by ship, plane, and sledging parties. This expedition successfully introduced two-way radio communication with the outside world and track vehicles, revolutionizing mapping and exploration. Planes were one of the greatest innovations. Though flying was often restricted by bad weather, this drawback was more than offset by the distances they could cover, the aerial perspective, and the information aerial photography could supply.

These achievements set the stage for the United States Navy's Operation High Jump at the close of World War II. Expeditions had now developed into costly government-funded exercises. In 1946–47 thirteen ships, twenty-three aircraft, and 4,700 personnel set up another base at Little America. Icebreakers were used for the first time and two groups working slowly around the continent mapped vast areas of coastline and the interior using aerial photography.

The rugged mountains, vast distances, blizzards, extreme cold, and short summers have been considerable barriers to the parties trying to explore the interior of Antarctica through the ages.

But the Americans did not have the Antarctic to themselves. Shackleton's dream of crossing the continent was finally accomplished in 1958 by the Commonwealth Trans-Antarctic Expedition led by Britain's Vivian Fuchs. A support team from New Zealand led by the conqueror of Mt. Everest, Sir Edmund Hillary, established the route from Ross Island to the South Pole using converted Ferguson farm tractors. Fuch's main party, which began at the Weddell Sea, reached the pole two weeks after Hillary and continued to the Ross Sea with the "Kiwi" party.

Governments soon began to take an interest in acquiring territory in the region. Britain made a formal claim on the Antarctic Peninsula and the Weddell Sea in 1908; New Zealand claimed what is now the Ross Dependency in 1923; and Australia made a claim to the region south of Australia explored by Mawson in 1933. France had already claimed Adélie Land in 1924, and the Australian claims fell on either side of France's. Norway formalized its claim in 1939. Each of these nations

recognized the claims of the others. Chile and Argentina, however, disputed Britain's claim to the Antarctic Peninsula as well as each other's claims, as they overlapped. These overlapping territorial claims still stand, though under the Antarctic Treaty such claims are held in abeyance.

The International
Geophysical Year (IGY)

Were it not for the scientists, the rivalries that marked the first years of Antarctic exploration and conflicting national claims that were a legacy of the explorers could well have turned Antarctica into a mosaic of colonial outposts, fragmented just as Africa and South America were in the eighteenth century.

The interest of the international scientific community in the Antarctic began with the First International Polar Conference held in 1879. This led to the First International Polar Year in 1882–83. This research was carried out mainly in the Arctic and subantarctic, and studies were conducted into the astronomy, optical phenomena, geomagnetism, meteorology, and natural history of the regions. The Second Polar Year was in 1932–33. In 1950, a third polar year was proposed to occur later in the decade so that it would coincide with a solar "maximum": a period when solar activity would be at its most intense. The year 1958 became known as the International Geophysical Year (IGY) and embraced the dual objectives of exploring outer space and the Antarctic. This massive cooperative effort in the name of scientific research laid the foundations for the Antarctic Treaty and led to the formation of an international Scientific Committee for Antarctic Research (SCAR). The latter is a non-government organization of scientists from some twenty countries that operates through ten permanent working groups relating to various scientific disciplines.

The Antarctic Treaty

In 1948 the United States first proposed that the Antarctic be ruled by a United Nations Trusteeship or by an eight-nation organization, but neither of these ideas caught on. It took sixty secret meetings to finally bring the nations concerned with the Antarctic to Washington, D.C., in talks aimed at having the continent set aside for peaceful scientific use only.

The Antarctic Treaty was finally signed on December 1, 1959, by the following twelve nations: Argentina, Australia, Belgium, Chile, France, Japan, New Zealand, Norway, South Africa, the Soviet Union, the United Kingdom, and the United States. It came into force on June 23, 1961, after it had been ratified by all parties. The treaty was comprised of fourteen articles (see appendices on page 130 for a summary) that the nations agreed upon for successful coexistence in the Antarctic.

Since then, twenty-seven other nations have become signatories. Seven of the original twelve nations were claimant states, but under the treaty all claims are held in abeyance and no new territorial claims can be submitted. The treaty has now been in place for thirty years and in this time it has served as an unprecedented example of international cooperation. The treaty bans any military activity or nuclear testing, and limits national programs to scientific research. Its sphere of interest includes all land and ice shelves south of 60°S. (The high seas north of latitude 60°S are subject to international law.) The treaty also ensures that the free exchange of information and scientists between countries can take place, and it gives nations the right to inspect the operations of other countries.

The thirty-nine countries that have become signatories to the Antarctic Treaty represent over 80 percent of the world's population, and include many developed and developing nations as well as the superpowers. There are several levels of membership of the Antarctic Treaty.

At present there are twenty-five full "Consultative Parties," nations that are engaged in substantial scientific research activity. This is usually interpreted as meaning that such nations maintain a year-round base on the continent. Among the Consultative Parties are the twelve original signatories and Brazil, China, India, Italy, Poland, South Korea, Sweden, Germany, Uruguay, and, most recently, Finland and Peru. There are an additional fourteen nonvoting nations, or "Non-Consultative Parties," which, though not conducting any substantial research, agree to ratify and abide by the terms of the treaty. These nations include Bulgaria, Canada, Cuba, Czechoslovakia, Denmark, Greece, Hungary, the Netherlands, Papua New Guinea, Romania, and Spain.

Since the treaty was signed, several other conventions have been completed, designed to protect Antarctic seals and conserve the living marine resources. There has also been progress in environmental protection with the "Agreed Measures," as they are known, which were first proposed in the 1960s by SCAR. Designed to give guidelines for expeditions operating in the Antarctic and to conserve Antarctic fauna and flora, these measures provided for several categories of protected areas and sites to conserve valuable scientific and biological features of the Antarctic. These include moss beds, fossil sites, bird colonies, and seal populations. The Agreed Measures also prohibit the introduction of any nonindigenous species to Antarctica and the killing or capture of any native mammal except where permits are issued for scientific research.

The Consultative Party nations meet every two years to negotiate the main business of the treaty, but there are other conferences designed to facilitate discussion about other conventions and issues. Contrary to what many believe, the Antarctic Treaty does not expire after thirty years. The treaty states that after the thirty-year period, which ends in 1991, amendments may be agreed upon by the majority of those present at the conference. If, within a two-year period after they have been tabled, any modifications are not acceptable to the treaty signatories, any signatory may withdraw two years after having given notice.

The most controversial issue that the Antarctic Treaty nations currently face is the so-called "Minerals Convention" (see Chapter Seven). This was an agreement concluded in 1988 among Antarctic Treaty nations, intended to regulate future mining and oil exploration in Antarctica. Other issues facing the treaty nations are the regulation of tourism and ways of enforcing the various Agreed Measures for the protection of flora and fauna.

The motives behind nearly a century of polar exploration have changed little in kind, only in degree. All ventures have more or less been undertaken not only for political ends (especially territorial claims) and the prospect of economic benefits to both the participating individuals and their home country, but also in the quest for scientific and geographical knowledge, a spirit of adventure and exploration, and a wish to experience the beauty of this wild and extreme environment.

Signposts on the research stations around the continent are a constant reminder of the remoteness of Antarctica and the international nature of its settlements.

Antarctic Wildlife:

Petrels, Penguins, and Seals

Many species of Antarctic wildlife are unique to the southern region of the world and little is known about them. Each of the major species that inhabit the Antarctic south of the convergence has a variety of adaptations that enable it to survive in this harsh environment. They all take their food from the sea and indeed most live at sea, although some breed on land. The major groups of fauna found in the Antarctic are birds (particularly seabirds and penguins) and mammals (seals and whales). Some species are found south of the Antarctic convergence, but they breed farther north on the warmer subantarctic islands, so they will not be looked at in any detail.

One of the most romantic and graceful of the birds that shipboard travelers to the Antarctic will see is the albatross. The extremely beautiful black-brown albatross feeds mainly on a diet of squid, and breeds on the subantarctic islands.

Birds

Although only eight species of flying birds breed on the continent itself, some thirty-five species breed in the latitudes south of the Antarctic convergence. These include pelagic species such as albatrosses and petrels and the skuas, gulls, cormorants, and terns that forage close to the shore.

One of the most romantic and graceful of the birds that shipboard travelers to the Antarctic will see is the albatross, the most famous being the
wandering albatross, which roams the Southern Ocean soaring effort-
lessly on the updrafts, seeming to stay aloft for days on end. The other
albatross species, all of which are extremely beautiful, include the light-
mantled sooty, and the gray-headed, the yellow-nosed, and the black-
browed albatross. There is believed to be a total of 750,000 breeding pairs
encompassing these six species of ocean wanderers. The albatross feeds
mainly on a diet of squid, and breeds on the subantarctic islands. The
adults share incubation, brooding, and feeding of the single chick.

There are four species of petrel in the Antarctic: the snow petrel, the
pintado petrel, the Antarctic petrel, and the Antarctic fulmar. All have
dense plumage and webbed feet. They feed at sea but remain closer to
the coast. The snow petrel, possibly the loveliest member of the family,
is pure white with black eyes and black underdown. It lives in the
Antarctic all year and can be found up to 435 miles (696 km) inland on
isolated nunataks.

The snow petrel, possibly the
loveliest of all the polar petrel species, is
pure white with black eyes and black under
down. They live in the Antarctic all year
round and can sometimes be found 160
miles (100 km) inland on isolated nunataks.

South polar skuas *(top)*, the raptors of the south, prey on injured penguins and chicks. Antarctic petrels *(bottom)* have dense plumage and webbed feet. They feed at sea but live closer to the coast, nesting in large colonies on high cliffs above the water.

Of the coastal birds there are two species of cormorant that are commonly found on the Antarctic Peninsula. As well, there are two species of sheathbill and one species of gull that are mainly restricted to the peninsula of the subantarctic islands.

Skuas and Southern giant petrels are the birds of prey of the Antarctic. There are two species of skua, the Antarctic and the brown, and both are very aggressive and similar in appearance. Should anything venture close to a skua's nest it will be swooped on every time. During the breeding season skuas nest on the continent and raise just one chick. Once the breeding season ends, however, they roam the oceans feeding on krill. During the summer they stake territories near penguin rookeries enabling them to easily raid eggs and chicks.

During the summer months the Antarctic tern breeds around the continent, particularly on the Peninsula, and on most of the Antarctic islands. Arctic terns also arrive in large numbers each summer to feed, flying some 25,000 miles (40,000 km) from their nesting grounds in the Arctic. Their migration is the greatest journey of any species of bird. To accomplish this incredible feat they fly day and night for eight months of the year.

Penguins

Penguins are the signature species of the Antarctic. They play the same role in the minds of the public as polar bears do in the Arctic. With their comical and endearing appearance and humanlike behavior, it is not surprising that penguins have become the favorites of cartoonists, illustrators, and photographers. In the wild, however, the pungent odor of a large penguin colony is much less appealing.

Penguins are flightless birds that have adapted to swimming in the sea and are thought to have evolved from petrellike flying birds some fifty million years ago. They have a very streamlined body and wings that function as flippers. These are used as paddles and their feet and stubby tails combine to form a rudder. Penguins are able to withstand the extreme cold because of the insulation provided by their densely packed feathers and a thick layer of blubber that also serves as an energy store. When a penguin swims, it does so in much the same manner as a porpoise, briefly shooting out of the water to catch its breath. At the same time its feathers become coated with a layer of air bubbles that help to reduce friction and also aid in insulation.

The Adelie is the smallest and most widely found penguin inhabiting the Antarctic. It is estimated that there are some five to ten million pairs of Adelies around the continent. Adults weigh twelve pounds (5.5 kg) and stand twenty-eight inches (71 cm) high.

Adelie penguins come ashore in October to breed during the brief weeks of summer. They form colonies on islands, beaches, and headlands all around the Antarctic coast. It is not unusual to see colonies of hundreds of thousands of birds.

There are three main groups of penguins found in the Antarctic proper: the brush-tailed, the crested, and the king and emperors (which comprise a single genus). The species most commonly associated with the Antarctic continent are the Adelie penguins (a member of the brush-tailed genus) and the much larger emperor penguins, both of which breed on the continent itself. There are also very large numbers of chinstrap penguins (also members from the brush-tailed genus) on the islands of the Antarctic Peninsula and around the continent, possibly some ten million pairs. Gentoo penguins are found over the widest range, appearing on the coastal islands as well as the cooler subantarctic islands.

The Adelie is the smallest and most broadly distributed penguin inhabiting the Antarctic. It is estimated that five to ten million pairs of Adelies inhabit the continent. Adults weigh 12 pounds (5.5 kg) and stand 28 inches (71 cm) high. For their size, the birds are well insulated against the rigors of cold and blizzards. Unlike the emperor penguin, which breeds on the continent during the winter, Adelie penguins come ashore in October to breed during the brief weeks of summer. Mating takes

place once the pair establish a rocky nest. The older birds tend to stake
out nesting sites in the middle of the colony where they are better protected from marauding skuas. There is fierce competition for nesting
sites, especially on higher, well-drained ground. In fact, stealing pebbles
from neighboring birds' nests is a favorite pastime.

   Adelie penguin colonies form on islands, beaches, and headlands all
around the Antarctic coast. The presence of groups of hundreds of thousands of birds is not unusual. The first eggs are laid in early November
and if the egg is left for more than an hour or two, it will cool and
become infertile. If nests are abandoned the eggs are easy prey for
skuas, the Adelie penguin's main enemy on land. The males and
females take turns incubating the eggs. The female returns to the sea
within hours of laying the egg, leaving the male alone for up to two
weeks while his partner feeds. Most pairs produce two eggs separated by
an interval of two to three days, and incubation takes about thirty days.
The two chicks hatch almost simultaneously. Inevitably, one chick is
stronger and consequently is able to win more food from its parents;
if food is scarce the second chick often dies.

The chicks are fed by whichever parent is present at the time. The chicks are brooded closely by their parents for the first two to three weeks and their appetite is considerable. Growing rapidly, the chicks soon develop a thick woolly gray down and quickly become almost as large as their parents. During the third or fourth week they join other chicks in crèches or nursery groups. This leaves both parents free to go to sea to feed sufficiently to satisfy their chicks' increasing demands. A parade of adults can regularly be seen moving between the colony and the sea. The birds congregate at the water's edge in large numbers waiting for the appropriate moment to take the plunge. The Adelie's main water predators are leopard seals, which often lie in wait beneath such a group to snare the first penguin into the water. By late March most Adelies have left the colonies to spend the winter in the comparative warmth of the offshore pack ice.

Adelie penguins provided generations of early explorers with entertainment, palatable eggs, and tough but tasty meat. Through detailed studies of the birds' breeding and eating behavior today, Adelie penguins are scrutinized by scientists as an indicator species to monitor the abundance of krill.

For their size, the Adelie penguins are well insulated against the rigors of cold and blizzards, but the chicks are more vulnerable *(below).*

The chinstrap penguin is slightly smaller than the Adelie and more aggressive. It is found mostly in the subantarctic, but large colonies also exist on the Antarctic Peninsula. Chinstraps have a distinctive band of black-tipped feathers under their chin, like the strap of a guardsman's helmet, giving them their name. Their breeding cycle and diet is similar to that of the Adelie penguin, and on the Antarctic Peninsula the two species often can be found breeding side by side.

The gentoo penguin (also a member of the brush-tailed genus) is slightly larger than the Adelie and chinstrap penguins, standing 30 inches (76 cm) tall and weighing 13 pounds (6 kg). They can be recognized by their orange beaks and the white markings above their eyes.

Following page: Adelie penguins spend the winter months on the relative warmth of the pack ice.

Emperor penguins are the largest and most biologically interesting of the southern species. Adults stand about 39 inches (1 m) tall and weigh up to 66 pounds (30 kg). There are some 350,000 of these regal and elegantly painted birds in thirty rookeries scattered around the continent — most of which are located on fast ice. The breeding pattern of emperor penguins differs from that of other penguin species because they breed through the winter. After three to five weeks of courtship, the female lays a single egg in May and then passes the egg over to her mate and goes to sea to feed. The male incubates the egg for another two months, holding it on top of his feet, where it is completely covered by a thick roll of skin and feathers. During this period the males huddle together for added warmth and protection against the bitter winds and subzero temperatures. By the time the female returns from feeding, the male will have lost up to a third of his body weight. The female then takes over for a six-week period, during which time the male goes to find food. Once the young hatch they join other chicks in a crèche that is protected by a few adults. By January the sea ice begins to break out, but by this time the chicks have shed their soft down and are able to fend for themselves. The emperors are believed to have developed this winter breeding pattern to allow the chick to grow to independence at a time when food is most plentiful. The adults are large enough to withstand the winter without regular feeding.

Above: The rockhopper penguin has prominent "eyebrow" feathers and occur mostly in the warmer subantarctic regions north of the limit of the pack ice. The king penguin *(right)*, the second largest of the penguins, also breeds only in the subantarctic. *Opposite page:* Emperor penguins are the largest and most biologically interesting of the southern species. Adults stand about three feet (1 m) tall and weigh up to sixty-six pounds (30 kg). There are some 350,000 of these regal and elegantly painted birds in thirty rookeries scattered around the continent.

Other species of penguins are found mostly in the warmer subantarctic regions north of the limit of the pack ice. These are the rockhopper, the macaroni (both of the crested genus), and the king penguin. The latter breeds on the South Georgia and South Sandwich Islands, while the macaroni can be spotted as far south as the South Shetlands. Rockhopper penguins do not breed south of Heard Island (53°S).

<Weddell seals live on or under the fast ice all year round and feed mainly on fish and squid.

Mammals

All Antarctic mammals are marine and they include twelve species of whales and five species of true or "earless" seals.

Seals

There are four species of seals indigenous to Antarctica: the Weddell, the Ross, the crabeater, and the leopard. Two more, the elephant seal and the fur seal, visit the continent every year. All Antarctic seals feed at sea using the enhanced sight of their large eyes. Each of the species has a different diet or feeds in a different region so there is little competition among them. The seal was the first Antarctic species to be commercially harvested, beginning as early as the 1820s. The trade in sealskins brought several species, including the Southern fur seal, close to extinction. Today, seals in the Antarctic are protected by the Convention for the Conservation of Antarctic Seals, which sets a quota for the number of specific species to be taken for science and commercial purposes.

Weddell seals live on or under the fast ice all year and feed mainly on fish and squid. These seals are most likely to be seen on the continent as they haul themselves onto the ice at tide cracks or rest beside breathing holes that they keep open with their teeth.

Some fifteen million crabeater seals are estimated to exist in the Antarctic. Despite their name they eat mostly krill, but this is supplemented by small fish and squid. Their teeth grow in rows—the upper and lower teeth interlocking like a strainer, enabling them to expel water while they retain their food. Crabeater seals are seldom seen on the coast as they spend most of their time in the pack ice offshore.

Ross seals are rarely seen on the continent as they, too, live on the pack ice and feed on squid. This has made studying the species very difficult.

Weddell seals are the most likely species to be seen on the continent as they haul out onto the ice at tide cracks.

The most ferocious of the Antarctic seals is the leopard seal, which can usually be seen cruising in the vicinity of penguin colonies. Females (larger than the males) grow up to 11½ feet (3.5 m) long and can weigh up to 1,100 pounds (499 kg). Their sharp teeth are well adapted for tearing apart the flesh of the penguins and other seals that constitute a large part of their diet, although they also hunt fish, squid, and krill. Leopard seals catch penguins by their feet and then beat them back and forth on the surface of the water to skin them. It has been calculated that there are some 220,000 leopard seals around the Antarctic and they are mostly seen on the pack ice during summer.

The Southern elephant seal does not breed in the Antarctic, but young males come ashore at various places around the continent. This seal species is the largest found in the Antarctic: the males are much larger than the females and can measure 20 to 30 feet (6 to 9 m) in length and weigh up to 4 tons (3.6 metric tons). Females only weigh up to 1 ton (.9 metric ton) and are usually no more than 11½ feet (3.5 m) long. The most notable feature of the males is the inflatable proboscis, which is particularly prominent in harem bulls, the main breeding males. The seals come ashore in various places to molt in December, January, and February, and lie around for weeks at a time in muddy depressions called wallows. Elephant seals feed mostly on fish and squid. Some 600,000 to 700,000 Southern elephant seals inhabit the Southern Ocean.

The Antarctic fur seal is found in the South Shetland, South Orkney, and South Sandwich Islands. The males grow to 7 feet (2 m) in length and weigh 300 pounds (136 kg); the females are much smaller. This species was decimated in the nineteenth century by British and American sealers who pursued them for their skins; over 320,000 pelts were taken from the South Shetland Islands within four years of their discovery in 1819. Other species were also severely plundered, although not for skins but for oil.

Opposite page: The lumbering southern elephant seal does not breed in the Antarctic, but young males come ashore at various places around the continent to molt in January and February. *Above:* Weddell seals keep their breathing holes open with their sharp teeth. Despite their appearance they are gentle when compared to the leopard seal *(below),* which are usually seen cruising in the vicinity of Adelie penguin colonies.

The striking hourglass dolphin is the only dolphin species that lives in the icy Antarctic waters.

Whales and Dolphins

The two main species of whales, baleen and toothed whales, are both found in the Antarctic. Baleen whales are usually larger and feed on plankton and krill, which they strain through sievelike plates. Toothed whales have rows of peglike teeth used to grasp and tear their prey of squid, fish, and octopus.

The largest animal ever to have lived is the blue whale, a baleen species that can exceed 90 feet (27 m) and weigh 150 tons (136 metric tons). The largest of the Antarctic toothed varieties is the sperm whale. Sperm whales are also the world's deepest diving mammal, able to reach depths of 1¼ miles (2 km). Only the bull (adult male) sperm whale inhabits the Antarctic, and then only in summer.

There are eleven other smaller species of toothed whales that inhabit the waters of Antarctica proper. The most notorious is the orca (the so-called killer whale), which feeds on seals, squid, and even some of the "great" whales. It is believed that most toothed whales do not stray far from their territories. Baleen whales, on the other hand, migrate over the entire globe, moving from the Antarctic, where they feed, to the subtropics, where they breed and spend the winter. The most well known of

these species is the humpback, which is frequently spotted since herds pass close to inhabited coastlines during their migrations.

Earlier in this century blue whales, Southern right whales, and humpbacks were nearly hunted to extinction, but they are now gradually recovering. Today an international ban on commercial whaling is in force, but the Japanese continue to hunt minke whales under the guise of scientific investigation. Whaling activities are monitored by the International Whaling Commission (IWC), but the smaller cetaceans—such as various species of dolphins—are not covered by the IWC or any other Antarctic regulation. Both minke and fin whales can still be regularly seen in the Antarctic. It is clear that the minke whale has benefited from the destruction of other Antarctic species, and has possibly even doubled in number. The minke was named after a whaler named Meineke who mistook one for a baby blue whale. The fin whale is the second largest whale species and it travels both in a group or alone.

All the main species of Antarctic wildlife are dependent on the ocean for their food. Thus it is important to understand the basis of their diet and the complex interrelationships of the ocean food chain.

Plankton to Lichens:

Antarctica's Ecosystems

Today Antarctica has a limited number of finely balanced ecosystems, most of which are marine based. On the continent itself, however, there are small areas around the fringes where the land is not permanently covered by ice. Often, these sites are home to lower forms of plant life—such as bacteria, lichens, and mosses—and minute animals. The freshwater and saline lakes found in the oases around the continent may also support relatively simple ecosystems. The great variations in climatic conditions on the continent prevent the establishment of higher plant and animal species, thus keeping the land-based ecosystems very simple.

British microbiologists at Australia's Davis Station examine plankton collected from one of the saline lakes in the Vestfold Hills.

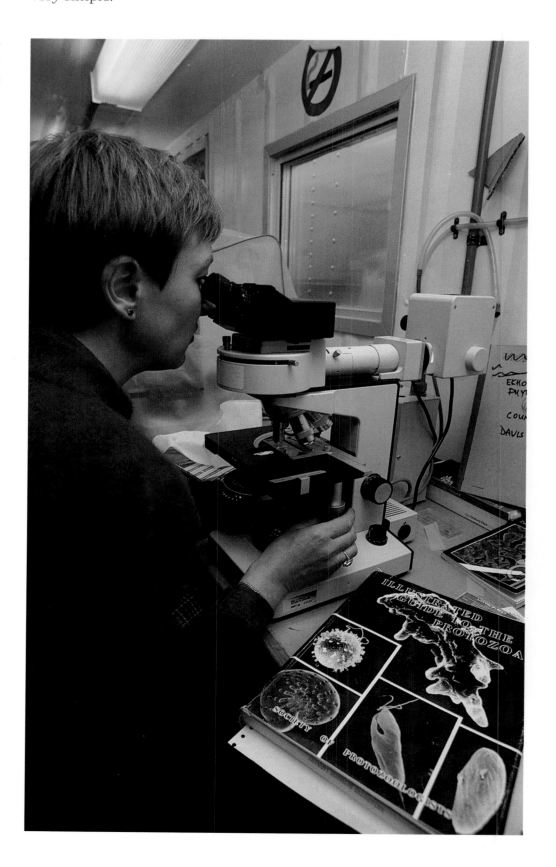

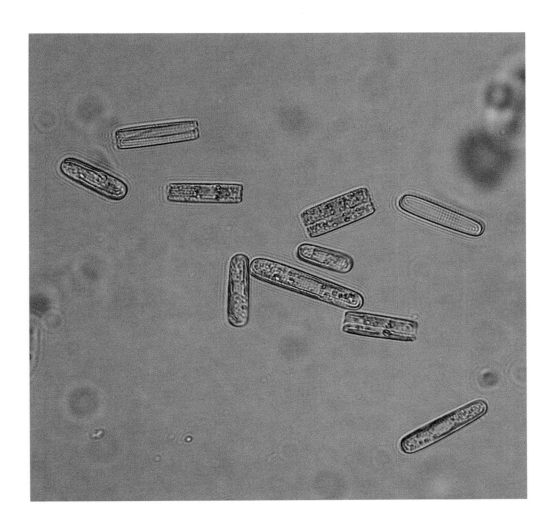

Plankton

Most life in the Antarctic begins in the ocean, and plankton is the foundation of the marine food chain. In the nutrient-rich waters south of the Antarctic convergence, phytoplankton and zooplankton (microscopic plants and animals) occur in profusion during the summer growing season. The rest of the year the lack of light and frequently heavy cloud cover, as well as the extensive pack ice, limit the productivity of the oceans.

Phytoplankton, which consist mainly of pelagic unicellular algae (free-swimming, single-celled algae), are minute drifting photosynthetic organisms. These creatures convert the energy of the sun into plant matter (chemical energy). Diatoms—a form of these single-celled plants —of which there are over 100 species, are a main component of the marine phytoplankton. Massive blooms of this organism are responsible for the green discoloration that occurs on the surface of the ocean on occasion. When these blooms occur the water can change from being crystal-clear to having the consistency of pea soup in a matter of days. Ice algae is often observed on the underside of pack ice when approaching the Antarctic by sea. When disturbed by a ship's passage it appears as a brown band or layer.

The next link on the food chain are zooplankton, which feed on phytoplankton. These include arrow worms, fish larvae, jellyfish, and small crustaceans, but the most significant and well-known zooplankton in the food chain is krill.

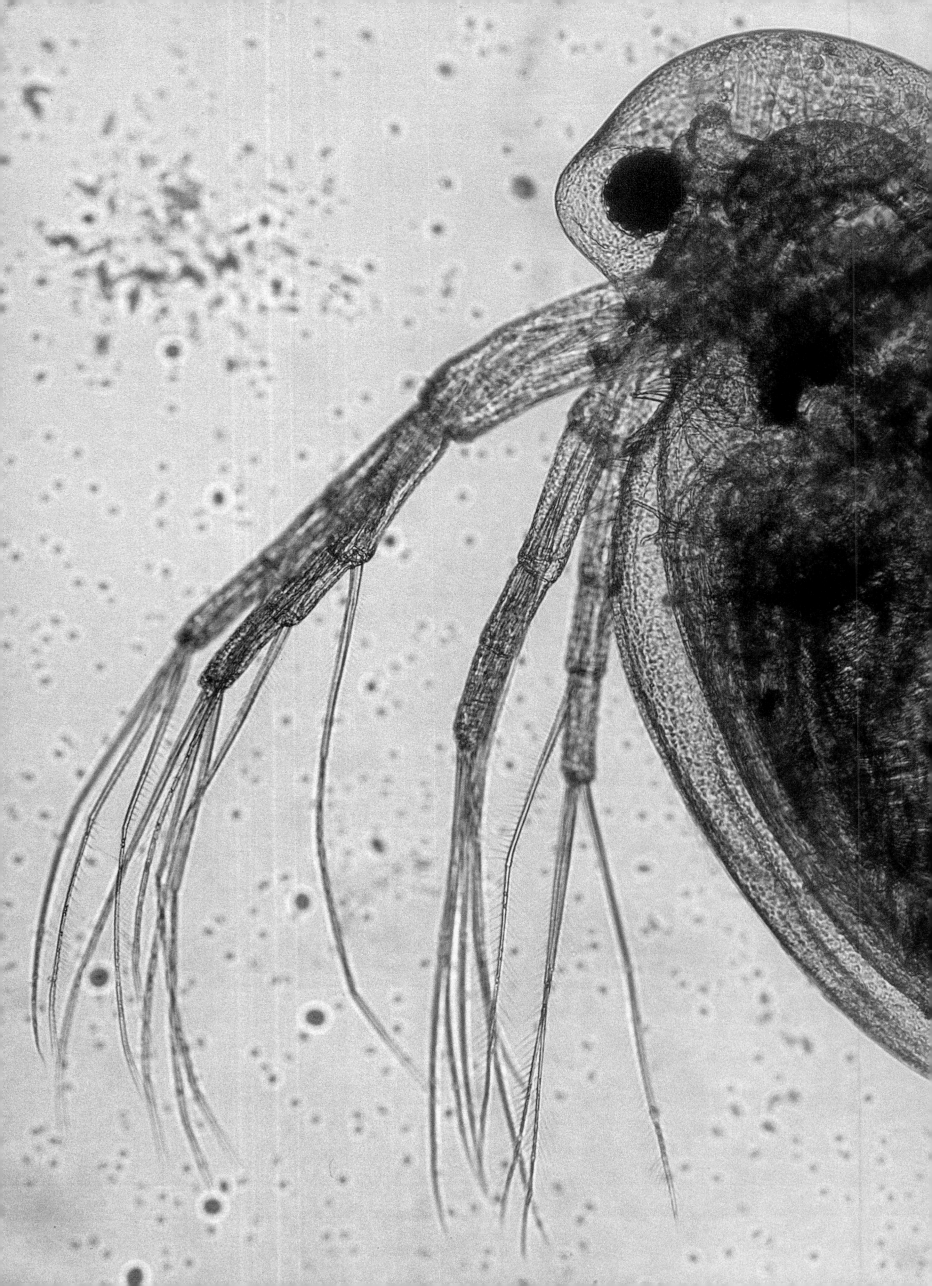

Krill

Krill are a shrimplike crustacean, about 2 to 3 inches (5 to 8 cm) long. Its name is derived from an ancient Norwegian word that once applied to larval fish and other tiny marine creatures. The term "krill" has also become a generic name used to describe other animals that baleen whales feed upon. Today, krill in Norwegian means whale food. The main species of Antarctic krill is *Euphausia superba,* but there are also ten other types. *Euphausia superba* is almost the sole diet of baleen whales in the Antarctic.

Despite the importance of these tiny crustaceans in the food chain, very little is known about their ecology or biology. In recent years, krill have been kept alive in laboratories, enabling more detailed study. Their behavior is fascinating. It is now known that krill either swim forward by using their five pairs of rear paddle-shaped legs or propel themselves quickly backward using their tails. They feed using another six pairs of forward legs, each of which is split into two branches and covered with a netlike array of feathery setae. These are used to gather tiny diatoms— the single-celled plants they graze on. Unlike most zooplankton, krill are heavier than seawater. To stay in one place they must constantly paddle, as though treading water.

Zooplankton, microscopic animals such as the crustacean *(opposite page),* are food for krill *(above),* the basis of the Antarctic food chain.

Antarctic krill spawn mainly in the summer months and adult females are able to lay between 2,000 and 3,000 eggs twice a year. These sink and hatch at depths of 2,300 feet (700 m). As the larvae grow they gradually rise toward the surface, taking two to three years to mature. Krill live from two to five years. As adults, they gather in huge swarms near the surface of the ocean, which is one of the reasons why they can be easily fished. They are also concentrated in particular areas around the continent often associated with eddies or gyres (upwellings of nutrient-rich bottom water). There is also a marked cycle of vertical movement of krill in the sea as part of their growth pattern. In winter they graze on algae growing on the underside of the pack ice. The krill also have a daily cycle. At night they rise to the surface but sink again during the daylight hours.

Krill are extremely rich in protein, which makes them attractive for commercial harvesting. The species was first seriously fished in the late 1970s, reaching a peak in 1982 when the catch was over 500,000 tons (454,000 metric tons). Ninety-three percent of this was taken by the Soviet Union. Other nations that fish for krill are Japan and, to a lesser extent, Chile, South Korea, and Poland. Today, the annual catch is around 400,000 tons (363,000 metric tons) annually. Over half the krill harvest is for nonhuman consumption—usually ending up as fish meal or animal feed. If it is for human consumption, krill must be processed within three hours of being caught. Otherwise, once the animal has died, its enzymes begin to break down the exoskeleton, allowing large concentrations of fluoride, which is harmful to humans in high doses, to build up in the flesh. Processed krill for human consumption is usually either minced, turned into a paste, or presented as fresh or canned tail meats.

It is believed that up to several hundred million tons of Antarctic krill exists, but this figure is based on the estimates of consumption by predators that are, at best, unreliable. Until the abundance and biology of this little known species is better understood, biologists remain concerned about the possibility of overfishing and thus causing enormous damage to the Antarctic food chain. Most higher species of flesh eaters or carnivores in the Antarctic (the penguins, seals, seabirds, fish, and squid as well as giant baleen whales) feed on krill. This makes the Antarctic marine food chain relatively simple, with krill as the key or central species. In the entire food chain there are only three or four levels of species from the basic photosynthetic organisms or primary producers—the phytoplankton—to the higher flesh-eating levels, which include species such as whales, seals, and birds. The top carnivores are the orca and leopard seals that feed on penguins, squid, and other seals. Because of their dependence on one food source the baleen whales would be very susceptible to changes in the krill stocks.

Human activity such as fishing is not the only potential threat to krill. Since phytoplankton is the main diet of the krill, this crustacean, and all

Night trawling for krill specimens to be used for scientific research also yields many other species of zooplankton.

the higher animals that feed on it, may be at risk if the suggested rise in sea temperatures (as a result of the greenhouse effect) alters the pattern of the phytoplankton blooms. In addition, krill is also believed to be threatened by the higher levels of ultraviolet light that now reach the Antarctic as a result of the thinning of the ozone layer over the continent each spring.

Squid and Fish

Antarctic squid and fish are the intermediate level of the food chain in the Southern Ocean. There is thought to be a stock of some 100 million tons (91 million metric tons) of squid in the Antarctic seas, and of this seabirds, seals, and whales are estimated to consume up to 34 million tons (31 million metric tons) per year. Squid are cephalopods, but little is known about their biology and ecology. There is considerable interest in commercial fishing for squid by the nations already catching krill in the Southern Ocean.

Of the Antarctic fin fish, some 200 species are found south of the Antarctic convergence, but only 25 percent of these are unique to the far south. Many species found in the polar latitudes have developed sophisticated mechanisms for surviving in very cold conditions. These include low metabolic rates, and having a form of antifreeze in their blood to maintain a higher rate of protein synthesis than would be expected.

The free-swimming or pelagic fishes were one of the first species harvested commercially after the decline of the whales. Some species of Antarctic fin fish, however, already have been overexploited, particularly the South Georgia cod, *Notothenia rossi.* As early as 1970–71, peak catches of over 500,000 tons (454,000 metric tons) were taken around South Georgia; these have since declined to the point where the fishery is no longer commercially viable. The stock of this species is now less than 2.5 percent of the original amount. Other species known to have been depleted are the Antarctic icefish *Champsocephalus gunnari.* The main fin-fishing nation in the Southern Ocean has been the Soviet Union.

As scientific programs focus more on the marine biology of the Antarctic, trawling and diving activities beneath the ice have begun to reveal unusual bottom-dwelling flora and fauna that have developed myriad adaptations to the environmental limitations of cold, low light, and a short growing season. The Antarctic seabed supports a great diversity of life, much more so than the Arctic, where there has been far less time for organisms to evolve the specialized adaptations necessary to survive. The number of land species in the Antarctic is far fewer and less well-developed than those that live on the sea floor.

During the summer months, concentrations of green algae develop in the nutrient-rich runoff areas of many Adelie penguin colonies.

Ecosystems on Land

Scientists have so far identified over 400 types of lichens and eighty-five kinds of mosses in Antarctica. Only two species of flowering plants (angiosperms), however, occur on the entire continent: a single grass species, *Deschampsia antarctica,* and a small cushion-forming plant or pearlwort, *Colobanthus quintensis,* both of which are restricted to the more temperate part of the Antarctic Peninsula. The Peninsula is also home to 200 lichen species. The oases, such as the dry valleys of Victoria Land or the Vestfold Hills, are also host to limited plant life such as lichens and mosses.

Antarctica's land-based ecosystems are, in most cases, very primitive. This makes it an ideal place to study the interrelationships between the various levels. During the short summer growing season, the presence of water determines where the lichens, mosses, and algae can survive. The lichens are a symbiosis between algae and fungi where they need each other to be able to survive. They are a pioneering or colonizing vegetation that have developed physiological or ecological adaptations to cope with the extremes of low temperatures and drought. Lichens tend to hide in cracks where snow collects on northern exposures. In even the harshest places algae and fungi have been found growing in minute crevices beneath the surface of light-colored, semitranslucent rocks, through which warmth and sunlight can penetrate.

Mosses and lichens occur mostly in areas where it is warmer and where water collects. Cracks in rocks with a northerly exposure are usually well colonized.

Above: The areas surrounding Adelie penguin colonies are some of the richest terrestrial floral environments in the Antarctic. *Opposite page:* Moss and lichen beds are often extremely slow growing and fragile. Any disturbance, such as a boot print, may still be seen years later.

The richest terrestrial floral environments in the Antarctic are in the soaks and runoff slopes on the fringes of penguin colonies. Sheets of green algae are hardy enough to survive the constant traffic of birds going to and from the colonies. Another biological oddity in the Antarctic is red snow. This is caused by red pigments in some green algae species that can survive in communities on the surface of the snow in areas around the coast.

Lichen and moss beds in Antarctica are very slow growing and any interference is usually long-lasting. A boot print on a moss carpet may still be seen years later.

No land vertebrates can survive Antarctica's harsh conditions. The continent's largest permanent inhabitant is a $1/2$ inch (.13 mm) long midge. Among the meager vegetation that does survive, some beetles, mites, and anthropods such as springtails may be found, particularly near penguin and petrel colonies, although one species of mite has been found within several hundred miles of the South Pole. While tiny insects such as nematode worms, rotifers, and mites occur in damper mosses and soils, most of the animal population is made up of microscopic protozoa (single-celled creatures).

While Antarctica contains nine-tenths of the world's fresh water, most of it is frozen throughout the year. There are some ice-free areas where fresh water does occur in summer in quantities from pools to small lakes. Many of these lakes are extremely saline as a result of progressive evaporation. This high salinity creates an environment that most life forms cannot survive in, although some phytoplankton and zooplankton have evolved ways for coping with these extremes. Biologists working in the dry valleys and oases regularly discover new species and unusual survival mechanisms.

Against the Elements:

Polar Living and Logistics

The Antarctic can be an extremely hostile place. Without insulated clothing, heated buildings, and every need brought in from the outside, humans could not survive in the icy wastes of the far south. Traveling to the continent by air and sea, living and working there, and moving from place to place necessitates a continual struggle against the elements. While modern materials and technology have facilitated sophisticated ways of coping with the environmental limitations, such solutions are usually very expensive and often prone to failure. Getting to and from the continent safely continues to be the first major undertaking of any government or private expedition to the far south.

Intercontinental Travel

Most Antarctic stations are very isolated throughout the winter. The pack ice prevents an approach from the sea, while the short daylight hours and bad weather limit air approaches. In an emergency, airborne evacuations are occasionally carried out by Soviet or United States planes, which, equipped with skis, land on makeshift ice runways. Long-range helicopters also have been used in conjunction with ships that stand off beyond the limit of the fast ice. The United States regularly conducts several late-winter flights to McMurdo Station in the first weeks of light (late August) to take in the summer's first scientists, support workers, mail, and fresh food, but these flights are the exception.

A number of nations have regular air-transport services to Antarctica during the summer months. Weather permitting, the United States Air Force, in conjunction with the New Zealand Air Force, schedules daily Lockheed C-130 Hercules or Galaxy Starlifter flights from Christchurch in New Zealand to McMurdo. At the beginning of the season the planes land at Williams Field on the Ross Ice Shelf, but landings later in the season shift to a second strip on the ice shelf, which, once it is prepared, can take wheeled aircraft.

The Soviet Union has the most comprehensive air transport system in the Antarctic. They operate a fleet of ski-equipped aircraft that circle the continent to resupply their far-flung network of bases.

The main aerial route to Antarctica is via South America. The Chilean Air Force flies C-130 Hercules aircraft from Punta Arenas to its Teniente Rodolfo Marsh Station on King George Island. The flight takes only two and a half hours. The Argentine military also operates Hercules C-130 and Twin Otter aircraft from Ushuaia, Argentina's southernmost city, to its largest base, Marambio, on Seymour Island. A private Canada-based airline, Adventure Network International, also flies from Punta Arenas, taking tourists and mountaineers to various locations on the peninsula. Its DC-6 aircraft flies to the Patriot Hills where there is a blue-ice runway capable of taking wheeled aircraft. From there ski-equipped Twin Otters fly on to other destinations such as Vinson Massif in the Sentinel Range and occasionally to the South Pole. Chile is also planning to establish a summer base at the Patriot Hills ice runway to further its territorial claims.

The British are building a crushed-rock runway (which can accept wheeled aircraft year round) at Rothera Station, while the French have been constructing a rock runway at Dumont d'Urville for over ten years. This latter project has led to strong protests from environmental groups, who argue that the leveling of several islands to create the French airstrip has disturbed Adelie penguins and could affect a nearby emperor penguin rookery.

Australia is attempting to establish intercontinental air service from Hobart, Tasmania, to a compacted-snow runway at Casey Station. This runway would be suitable for a Hercules aircraft to land on.

Helicopters are extensively used on the Antarctic to deploy field parties (above).

A landing barge is hemmed in by pack ice during the resupply of the Chinese base, Jong Shan, in the Larsemann Hills.

The Soviets, however, have the most comprehensive air-support system in Antarctica. Most Soviet stations, including Molodezhnaya where there is a compressed-snow runway, and Mirnyy, can be approached by air, and a fleet of ski-equipped planes regularly circle the continent servicing the Russian bases. The flight from the Soviet Union to Antarctica takes just twenty-four hours, whereas the journey by ship can take up to six weeks.

Despite the increasing role of aircraft, most Antarctic stations are still supplied and serviced either partially or solely by sea. Most ships venturing to the Antarctic today have much-improved hull designs and propulsion to cope with the obstacle of pack ice that once bedeviled polar navigators. To be able to proceed through fast ice or push aside pack ice, a strengthened bow with a specially designed hull and very powerful engines is necessary. True icebreakers such as the United States Coast Guard vessels *Polar Star* or *Polar Sea* are capable of plowing through a 6 foot (2 m) thickness of pack ice at up to three knots powered by 60,000 shaft horsepower gas-turbine engines. When ramming the ice, or using their curved bow to ride up on top of it, these ships are capable of breaking ice 21 feet (6 m) thick. Many ships are ice-strengthened and are designed to be forced up over the ice rather than pinched under pressure. Even ice-strengthened ships can sometimes run into difficulties. While they are not in any danger of being crushed, if they become immobilized by pack ice, they are unable to avoid the paths of icebergs that are driven by sea currents rather than by the winds that move the pack ice around.

Icebreakers are very expensive to operate and only the larger nations such as Japan, the United States, and the Soviet Union can support vessels dedicated to such tasks. These ships are usually operated by coast guards or their navies. Instead of icebreakers most countries own or charter multipurpose ships that accommodate research facilities, can carry cargo, and have helicopter decks as well as moderate icebreaking capacity.

Most year-round bases in the Antarctic receive their first resupply each summer by helicopters that operate from ships that stand off at the edge of the fast ice, usually 30 to 40 miles (48 to 64 km) away. While the sea ice is still strong enough early in the summer season, some supplies are occasionally ferried ashore using vehicles or tractors towing cargo sleds. Apart from the extra distance, this is relatively convenient because the ice edge makes a natural deep-water port. However, storms and swell can cause unexpected breakouts of sea ice, and occasionally supplies have had to be rescued from ice that came adrift. No Antarctic stations have deep-water docking facilities, so when the sea ice has broken out or been opened up by icebreakers, the cargo ships move as close as possible to the shore and any supplies are unloaded into lighters, barges, or pontoons and then ferried ashore. Large quantities of fuel are required to heat and power Antarctic scientific research stations. Supplying the bases with fuel requires complex logistic support that often includes large tankers, pipelines, and storage facilities. This need for such a sophisticated system of transportation to get fuel to the stations is one of the reasons that most bases are located on the coast. Fuel is usually transported ashore by barge or, if the vessels can maneuver close enough to shore, via long flexible hoses that are run out from the resupply ships.

Getting materials from ship to shore is a constant problem in the short Antarctic summer.

Research Bases

Approximately twenty-five countries maintain research bases in Antarctica. The most concentrated collection of bases is located on the Antarctic Peninsula, with the remainder of bases mostly positioned around the perimeter of East Antarctica.

Research stations are usually situated on rocky outcrops immediately on the coast or in snow-free oases. The Chinese station, Jong Shan, Progress II, a Soviet scientific station, and the Australian Law Base, for example, are all located in the Larsemann Hills, one of the larger oases in eastern Antarctica. Australia's Davis Station, one of that country's three year-round research facilities, lies on the edge of the Vestfold Hills, another oasis.

Stations built on the ice cap or ice shelves, such as the Amundsen-Scott U.S. Base at the South Pole and the British Halley Base, are designed not only to cope with being buried by drift snow but with the slow but constantly shifting ice cap beneath them. Even so, they still have to be replaced at regular intervals. Halley has been rebuilt four times since it was established in 1956.

Regardless of where the bases are constructed around the continent, the precise shape and positioning of the buildings is crucial to avoid being covered by drift snow. Wind tunnel tests are sometimes used to establish the best designs. The danger of fire is another major factor in the design and construction of these stations. The air in Antarctica is so dry that timber becomes highly flammable. With only relatively small water supplies available, fighting fires becomes difficult. Therefore, buildings are generally spaced far apart to minimize the possibility of a blaze spreading. Most also have elaborate, automatic fire-fighting protection systems.

The dispersed nature of the facilities on the larger bases has certain drawbacks. Moving from building to building during blizzards can be hazardous, especially in winter when strong drift and whiteout conditions can prevail. Individuals have been known to get lost moving within the confine of a base. Some bases maintain special walkways with rails or ropes that are used as "blizzard lines" in extreme weather.

Most Antarctic stations are run and staffed by independent national research bodies, but some bases, such as those of France, Chile, and Argentina, are operated solely by the military of those countries. Most other nations, however, utilize military personnel in some areas of research, support, or logistics.

Many countries maintain networks of facilities that are occupied only during the summer.

The first permanent nongovernment station established in Antarctica is on Ross Island. Called World Park, it was set up by Greenpeace in 1987 as an example of a low-impact research station. It was begun as a part of a campaign to gain observer status to the various Antarctic Treaty institutions, as well as to focus world attention on the need for conservation in Antarctica. Greenpeace's environmental research on Ross Island has detected high levels of PCBs and other pollutants emanating from nearby bases. Their presence has emphasized the need for other national expeditions to make a greater effort to minimize their impact.

Greenpeace resupplies its permanent base on the Ross Island with its own ship.

Indeed, waste and garbage of every kind pose an increasing problem in Antarctica. Many countries now follow a policy of storing all solid waste from their bases so that it can be shipped to disposal facilities back home. This is an extremely costly, but essential, exercise. In times gone by refuse from Antarctic stations was collected and buried in landfills. Today combustible material is usually disposed of in high-temperature incinerators. However, the disposal of human waste is an ongoing problem as the low temperatures hinder normal decomposition. In an attempt to cope with this problem, Australia's Davis Station, for example, uses gas-fired toilets, but these, too, pose a problem as potential fire hazards. As the number of stations and visitors to the Antarctic increase, so do the environmental problems.

The combined staffs of the twenty-five nations that operate in the Antarctic number some 4,000 people who spend either all or part of the year in the far south. Hundreds more, as official observers, politicians, filmmakers, artists, and journalists, make the round-trip to the continent every year on the government resupply ships and aircraft.

Progress 2, in the Larsemann Hills, is one of the eight year-round bases the Soviet Union maintains in Antarctica.

The Soviet Union maintains the largest number of stations; eight manned year-round and four others occupied only during the summer. The coldest and most remote of these stations is Vostok, located at the "pole of inaccessibility," the most remote point in the Antarctic. The other permanent Soviet stations are Molodezhnaya, Mirnyy, Novolazareskaya, Bellingshausen, Leningradskaya, Russkaya, and Progress II.

The United States maintains four permanent stations including the largest, McMurdo: In summer it may be home to over 950 people, and during the winter it supports 130. McMurdo is, in effect, a small town, with its own theater, chapel, radio station, bars, and elaborate scientific laboratories. It is also just 2 miles (3 km) from New Zealand's Scott Base. The Amundsen-Scott U.S. base at the South Geographic Pole is located inside a large geodesic dome that is built beneath the ice and houses eighty people in the summer. Because the ice cap moves at 33 feet (10 m) each year, the station was built away from the pole itself. It is now actually one-fifth of a mile from the South Geographic Pole. By the year 2020 it will be exactly over the South Pole because of the movement of the ice cap. The other year-round U.S. stations are Palmer, on Anvers Island on the Antarctic Peninsula, and Siple, in Ellsworthland at the head of the Peninsula.

On King George Island nine countries maintain research bases, due more to its proximity to South America (600 miles; 960 km) than to any particular scientific research potential. The nations represented at these stations are Argentina, Brazil, Chile, China, Peru, Poland, South Korea, the Soviet Union, and Uruguay. The Chilean station is actually a colonial outpost, boasting its own bank, post office, school, hospital, and a population of up to 240 people that includes a number of families stationed there on two-year tours. Such are the Chilean efforts to bolster its territorial claim to Antarctica.

Argentina has a similar program at its Marambio and Esperenza stations on the Antarctic Peninsula, where men, women, and children winter each year. In fact, eight children were born at Esperenza in the years between 1978 and 1983. The first baby born in Antarctica was Emilio Marcars Palma at Marambio in 1978, getting Argentina's policy of colonizing Antarctica off to a start. Like Chile's station on King George Island, Marambio is more like a frontier settlement than a scientific base.

Deception Island, created by an ancient volcanic eruption, once housed British and Chilean bases as well as a British whaling station. However, substantial eruptions in 1967, 1969, and 1970 destroyed the bases and they were abandoned. Thousands of whales were once slaughtered in the water around the island, but all that remains today are the ruins of the ships and the whaling station. The island is still a popular port of call for cruise ships. Tourists from these ships regularly bathe in the warm, and in some places boiling hot, waters of the lagoon that now fills the caldera, the large crater formed by the eruption. Not all Antarctic stations feature such comforts!

There is a strong feeling of international camaraderie among expeditioners living in the Antarctic.

Some of the other substantial stations around the perimeter of the continent that are maintained for consultative party status and scientific research objectives are: Japan's Syowa Base on the Prince Olav coast; the French Dumont d'Urville Station on the Adélie Coast; India's Dakshin Gangotri on the Princess Astrid Coast; South Africa's Sanae Base on the Jelbartisen Ice Shelf; and Germany's George Base and Georg von Neumeyer Base on the Ekstrom Ice Shelf. No matter where they are located all bases in the Antarctic face similar transportation problems on the continent itself.

Transportation

Antarctic transportation has continually improved since Scott's day when man-hauling or the use of Manchurian ponies and husky dogs were the only options available for travel overland. Today, air, sea, and over-snow vehicles have become vital components in every nation's research efforts. In the summer season aircraft and helicopters are the main means of deploying field parties over long distances. For fieldwork on the ground, most countries use track vehicles with cabins, plus snow-mobiles and skidoos. For heavy tractor trains containing cargo (sleds), accommodation caravans, and fuel tankers, traction comes mainly from

Tracked vehicles, such as the "Weasel," are the main means of crossing icy terrain on the continent.

modified caterpillar tractors and giant snow-cats. In the areas around scientific stations during the summer, regular four-wheel-drive vehicles and three- or four-wheeled balloon-tire motorbikes are often used on graded roads. For the limited work which is performed during the winter, glaciologists mostly use tractor trains.

Some countries try to minimize the amount of vehicular traffic through snow-free areas and oases, since roads disturb the local ecology significantly both by their construction and by the pollution and dust caused by the vehicles. Even traditional forms of over-snow transportation are not without their problems. Husky dogs are no longer kept at New Zealand's Scott Base because of the damage they did to the wildlife whenever they broke from their traces or got out of control when sledging.

There are still two or three stations that run dog teams, but they are maintained more for recreational and historical reasons than as a practical means of transportation. While the dogs at Australia's Mawson Station are used for extended trips on the sea ice during winter, at the height of summer they are usually just run for sport near the base. Great Britain and Argentina also have dog teams, but they are gradually being phased out as a viable means of transportation as opposition from scientists and environmentalists increases.

With magnetic compasses unreliable because of the proximity of the South magnetic pole field, parties are constantly having to check their location. *Following page:* Scientific field parties and mountaineers in the Antarctic have to be prepared to sit in their tents for up to a week at a time because of high winds and bad weather.

There is a high level of interaction and cooperation among the countries operating in the Antarctic. Soviet geophysicists *(above)*, New Zealand biologists *(below)*, Chinese glaciologists *(opposite page, top)*, and Australian base leaders *(opposite page, below)* are all united against the common foe—the elements.

Life in the Antarctic

While there are considerable differences in the facilities and style of operation of the various stations, there are strong similarities in the types of individuals who are attracted to work in the Antarctic. There is in fact a shared consciousness among Antarctic veterans that has been evident from the earliest days of polar exploration. Australian Antarctic pioneer Douglas Mawson expressed such sentiments in a poem he wrote to Tannatt Edgeworth David:

> *And if perchance you hear the silence calling,*
> *The frozen music of star-yearning heights,*
> *Or, dreaming, see the seines of silver trawling*
> *Across the ship's abyss on vasty nights,*
> *You may recall that sweep of savage splendour,*
> *That land that measures each man at his worth,*
> *And feel in memory, half fierce, half tender,*
> *The brotherhood of men that know the South.*

Modern Antarctic research stations are luxurious compared to the primitive conditions that the pioneers of the Heroic Era endured. The most important change being that the permanent accommodation and research facilities are usually centrally heated.

A popular misconception about Antarctica is that the weather is always uncomfortable. Actually, calm summer days can be quite balmy, especially in more northern locations along the coast. Although the temperature can fall below zero, this alone need not be too unbearable; it is

the wind that causes the greatest discomfort. Yet the cold is not the only disruptive factor of living in the Antarctic year-round: In the depths of winter almost continual darkness frequently disturbs people's sleeping routines, adding to the physical stress of polar living. Insomnia is common and is sometimes known as "big eye." Thus many scientists adopt working hours that suit the particular needs of their research projects: For example, physicists studying aurora will work through to the small hours of the so-called night.

Facilities that help to encourage a more typical lifestyle are generally considered very important on bases. Many different crafts and hobbies, such as photography, listening to music, and amateur radio, are often pursued. Visits to field huts, skiing trips, and dog sledging are also provided at some stations for recreation. Some governments, however, restrict outdoor activities away from the station to minimize the risk of accidents and the potential for disaster should parties or individuals become lost in bad weather. Servicing field facilities, scientific research, and monitoring programs are the main legitimate ways of escaping the confines of larger government stations that may be constrained by the workings of bureaucracy and restrictive regulations.

Today, mountaineers and field workers in Antarctica enjoy the benefits of lightweight, synthetic insulating materials and scientifically designed clothing, but sled hauling and snow camping is still an arduous business.

Scientific and maintenance personnel generally work in Antarctica in seasonal shifts. The summer staff arrive early in the season and are ferried ashore by helicopter or arrive on the very first flights along with the mail and fresh food. Many of these workers leave on the last possible vessel at the end of the season. The staff that stay during the winter generally arrive in December or January, before the sea ice builds up.

During the summer, much of the scientific work is carried out away from the main bases, either during short field trips or at remote camps that develop, from necessity, into small villages. Today, remote field parties are well supplied and are usually deployed by ski-equipped aircraft or helicopters. They enjoy the benefits of synthetic materials and scientifically designed garments, camping gear, and rations. Downfeather- and Dacron-filled sleeping bags have replaced the heavy reindeer-skin bags of Scott's era, and fiberglass domes—called "apples"—are just one of the innovative forms of accommodation that field parties now often use in place of the more traditional pyramid tent. At the end of the summer season these remote field camps are closed up for the winter and then sometimes reoccupied the next season, or they may be removed entirely to be redeployed the following season to a new location.

The year-round research stations in Antarctica have to be completely self-sufficient, so the larger bases, with hospitals, services, and recreation facilities, become more akin to frontier villages. Most countries have modern stations with excellent living quarters where most physical needs are cared for. Today, psychological stresses are provided for, too.

Isolation always has been the main problem for winter staff. Separation from friends and family and from the events of the world beyond the continent can cause loneliness and even anxiety. Telegrams and high-frequency radio telephone links were once the only means of communication with the outside world, but these days mail arrives aboard supply and research ships. There are also satellite, telephone, fax, and computer links that help to reduce the sense of remoteness. Still, "winterers" must rely on their own company and that of their fellow base members. For this reason well-formulated stations often develop their own social schedules with weekly film nights, monthly theme parties, and big celebrations to mark such events as Midwinter's Day, the winter solstice, which ushers in the return of the sun to the dark continent.

Most countries have few, if any, women spending the winter in Antarctica on their research stations. Chile and Argentina are the exceptions, since the presence of families at these bases is part of their strategy of colonization to try and reinforce and publicize their territorial claims. Australia and the United States also have increasing numbers of women in various capacities from doctors to technicians, scientists, and occasionally station leaders. In the summer the male/female ratio at many other research stations usually becomes a little more balanced.

Spending a winter in Antarctica is, to most, an unthinkable prospect, but for some it is an experience they cannot wait to repeat. Some scientists and support staff have made careers of living in the Antarctic, with a number spending up to ten seasons on the continent, and there are a few who have returned for up to twenty or more seasons.

Recreation on the Antarctic research bases takes many forms—from ice yachting to skiing. However, the problems of accidents from the likes of crevasses and breakouts of the sea are ever-present; for this reason many countries limit the scope of the activities of their research expeditioners.

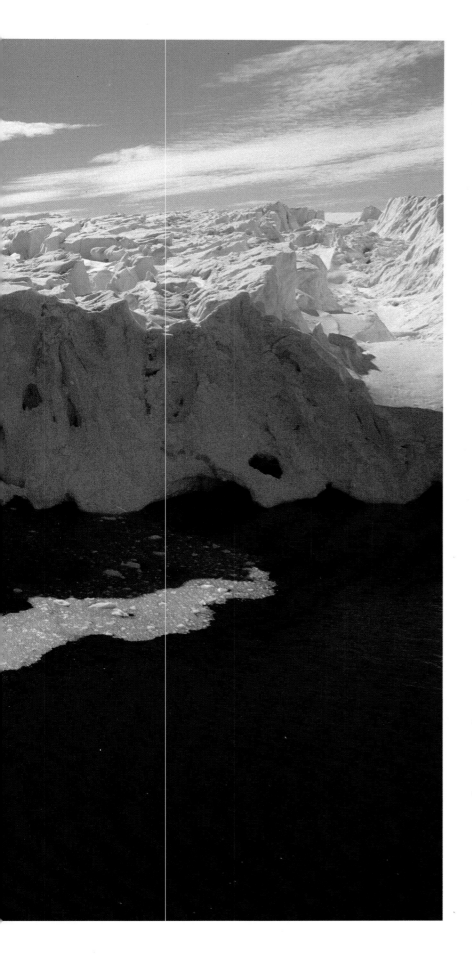

The Future:

Antarctica's Importance to the World

The future of Antarctica is regarded by many as being an issue of great importance to the world for a variety of reasons. Its value as a site for monitoring weather patterns, global temperatures, the upper atmosphere, and levels of pollutants is enormous. Antarctica is also a storehouse of detailed information about the world's past climate, geology and biology, and geophysical processes. Furthermore, Antarctica is the only place in the world where many varied and original scientific research projects can take place.

Of equal importance are the political considerations and wilderness values that are at stake with regard to the future of the Antarctic. The concept of maintaining at least one continent on earth free from the ravages of human exploitation and interference is of growing importance to many individuals, organizations, and even some countries. The continuation of the Antarctic Treaty System, especially the preservation of the articles (see appendix on page 130), is considered vital to the stability of the region and the continued peaceful coexistence of the nations who have an interest in the continent.

Provided it is well managed, increased ship-based tourism could be a positive development for the region. Potentially it may help to create a more powerful international lobby and public voice against mining. In the ongoing international debate between conservationists and pro-mining nations there are a diverse range of philosophical and ethical positions. The scientific value, however, provides the most universally accepted and powerful reason to conserve Antarctica in its unspoiled state.

Deep drilling for ice cores at Law Dome.

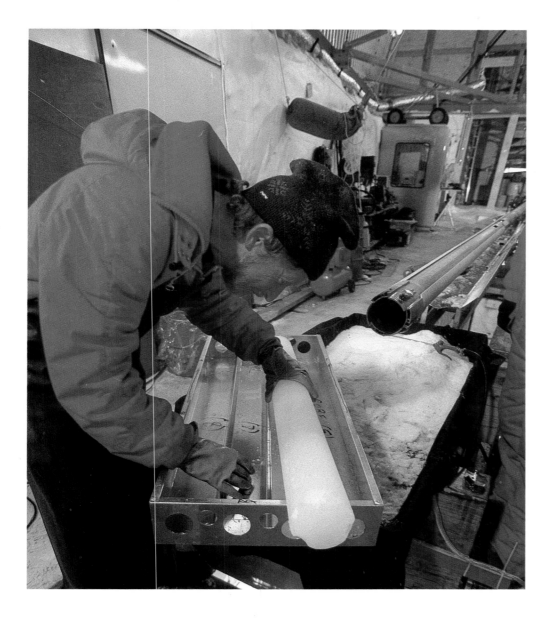

Information about the world's climate over the last 1,000 years can be obtained from the analysis of drill cores that are taken from deep in the ice cap.

Scientific Research

Scientific research conducted in the Antarctic is extremely wide-ranging. The atmosphere, continent, and seas of Antarctica constitute one of the world's greatest natural scientific laboratories. The research carried out in the Antarctic covers areas as diverse as solar wind, plasma physics, weather phenomena, the study of a wide range of organisms (including krill, whales, fish, seabirds, and plants), the survival of life forms at low temperatures, and the impact of man on a pristine environment. The earth science disciplines, glaciology, meteorology, and geology, as well as the biological and marine sciences, are at the core of most countries' research priorities. In addition, there are many specific programs that are the subject of multinational cooperative efforts, developed in accordance with the Scientific Committee on Antarctic Research (SCAR). These committees are built around subjects that must be looked at on a global level. For example, the committee addresses such subjects as the role of krill in the Antarctic food chain and the aerial mapping of the polar ice cap using ice radar.

At the other end of the spectrum there are many specific examples of the importance of research and the role that much smaller scale monitoring programs can play.

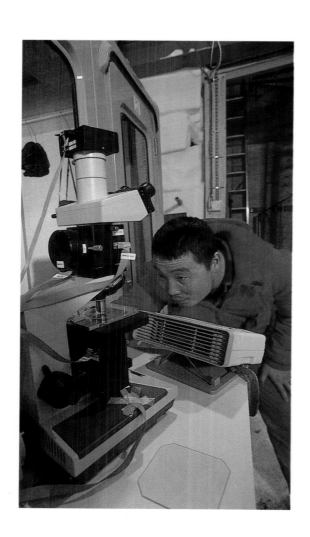

Glaciologists can extract the gases trapped within ice cores and compare it to the seasonal layering to date the various levels *(top)*. The crystal structure of ice cores can be analyzed on-site with the aid of polarized light *(below)*.

The thinning of the ozone layer above Antarctica, which now occurs each southern spring, was first recognized as a result of a regular monitoring of the upper atmosphere at a British research station on the Antarctic Peninsula. It was some years before the researchers were sufficiently confident of their results to announce their controversial findings to the scientific community, but the link between the ozone breakdown and chlorofluorocarbons had already been established. This research into ozone depletion continues to be most effectively studied in Antarctica.

Contained in the gases trapped in the layers of the Antarctic ice cap is a history of the earth's temperatures over the last 100,000 years. They reveal levels of carbon dioxide that can be calculated to determine ancient weather patterns. Deep-core drilling is being carried out by several countries including Australia, the United States, and France to discover these past climatic patterns.

Antarctica has also become important in the study of meteorites. The movement of the ice sheet and its subsequent ablation in certain locations has led to the discovery of concentrations of moraine (rock debris), which tend to contain a very high proportion of meteorites. In the last two decades over 7,500 meteorite fragments have been found on the continent. Some of these have been very unusual stony meteorites believed to have originated from Mars. Some meteorites contain amino acids, which are evidence that organic materials existed in the solar system more than 100 million years ago.

Not all scientific research programs in the Antarctic are equally valid or productive—for the very reasons many nations are there in the first place. To be a Consultative Party in the Antarctic Treaty System, nations are required to be engaged in so-called substantial scientific research activities, as discussed in Chapter Three. This is usually interpreted as maintaining one or more research bases on the continent. The quality

Biologists pump warm water into Adelie penguins to examine their stomach contents and determine the birds' feeding patterns. Adelies are also fitted with radio transmitters so scientists can plot their foraging patterns.

and quantity of research, however, is extremely varied. Among the Antarctic Treaty nations the more research that is conducted, the higher each country's prestige and international lobbying power is. Notwithstanding this international competition, there is an extremely high level of cooperation between the scientists of all nations working on polar projects.

The Antarctic research effort is far from evenly distributed. Where there are many scientific stations located in close proximity, such as on King George Island (where there are currently ten bases), research may be duplicated. For example, multiple meteorological reports from the same site are of little value, especially when no comparable information is available for the major part of Antarctica.

Polar Politics

The Antarctic Treaty System has been, and continues to be, a very important world diplomatic forum that has helped manage the only continent on earth that is "owned" by no one. The treaty has kept the Antarctic free from nuclear weapons and military activity and has greatly encouraged international cooperation. Even during periods of enmity, such as the Falklands-Malvinas war, the treaty nations (Great Britain and Argentina) engaged in it maintained a dialogue about Antarctica. The Antarctic could well be the model that demonstrates how the world can peacefully organize its political affairs in other international situations and in future arenas such as space.

The unifying effect that the debate on the future of the Antarctic has had on international conservation organizations is also significant. The 1990s could be seen as a most crucial decade in terms of how humans begin to reassess their role on the earth. The Antarctic may well be the psychological linchpin in this revolution. The possibility that the Antarctic may be saved from the activities of mining companies and eventually fall under the jurisdiction of a conservation regime could inspire concerned citizens to believe that many other far-reaching global problems,

Inevitably, the construction of bases and field stations for scientific research programs has an impact on the Antarctic environment *(above)*. Pollution also comes from the burning of waste *(below)* and the dumping of rubbish *(opposite page)*. However, high-temperature incinerators are now being used and solid waste is being collected and shipped back to its country of origin.

such as greenhouse emissions, might also be tackled and overcome in a spirit of international cooperation. Any breakdown in the Antarctic Treaty could lead to competition for Antarctica's resources along with a loss of cooperation between scientists and member nations. This, coupled with the potential for military activity, could lead to armed conflict that would have dire political consequences. The political importance of Antarctica can in no way be underestimated.

Wilderness

"In wilderness is the preservation of the world."

Thoreau

It is said that mankind needs to maintain a close link with nature for spiritual fulfillment. As the last unspoiled continent on earth, many believe that Antarctica is worth keeping relatively untouched for its pristine nature alone. The threats to the continent, however, come at all levels: global, regional, and local.

Changes in global physical factors stand to have significant and potentially far-reaching effects on the Antarctic. So-called greenhouse gases — carbon dioxide, methane, nitrous oxide, and the chlorofluorocarbons — are so named because they allow sunlight (shortwave radiation) to enter the atmosphere, but then trap the long-wave radiation given off by the earth. Thus the gases act just like a greenhouse and help to warm up the atmosphere. A change in the composition and amount of these gases is believed to have a long-term effect on the earth by raising the mean temperature. While this will affect the Antarctic ice cap (as discussed in Chapter One) in the short term by increasing the amount of snowfall, in the longer term it will lead to increasing flow rates of the ice cap and so generate more icebergs.

Krill, and all the higher animals that feed on them, are also believed to be at risk from the predicted associated rise in sea temperatures (also a result of greenhouse warming), and from the higher incidence of ultraviolet light due to the thinning of the ozone layer over the Antarctic.

Global pollution has already had an impact on Antarctica, particularly through nuclear fallout, which is present in the upper levels of sediments and ice cores retrieved during geological and glaciological expeditions.

At a regional level the possibility of mining, particularly drilling for oil in the continental shelf surrounding the Antarctic, is a very real threat. The technology for drilling in extreme conditions has been developed on the north coast of Alaska, so if the price of oil was to rise for a sustained period, then exploration for oil in Antarctica could become economically viable. The potential damage to the environment from oil spills caused by shipping accidents and the likelihood of damage to drilling rigs, production platforms, and pipelines as a result of the movement of icebergs makes such exploitation problem-ridden. The question of who should benefit from resource extraction from a continent that no one owns is another area fraught with potential problems.

Ill-conceived scientific research activities are also a threat to the Antarctic environment. Poorly managed bases and programs could have a lasting effect on specific areas through pollution from ships sinking or accidentally discharging oil, or from tanks leaking, as well as air pollution from the exhausts of power plants, vehicles, and aircraft.

Antarctic wildlife is also potentially threatened by introduced diseases. Now there are restrictions on many biological products, and even hydroponics is banned on some stations. The possibility of a poultry virus, known as Newcastle disease, that would affect penguins is sufficiently real in the Antarctic to make stringent handling procedures necessary for any poultry products such as eggs and frozen chickens that are taken south.

The Antarctic's marine ecosystems are already suffering from human activities quite apart from pollution. Despite the creation of the Convention for the Conservation of Antarctic Marine Living Resources (CCAMLR), dangerous depletion of several species of fin fish has resulted from overfishing (as discussed in Chapter Five).

Tourism

Antarctic cruise ships and air tours currently carry an estimated 2,000 tourists to the continent each summer. In a place where there has never been a native people, nor permanent inhabitants, everyone, strictly speaking, is a tourist. Individuals who pay to join an organized cruise are unquestionably tourists. Mountaineers and sailors who venture to the Antarctic on private yachts and chartered planes in ever-increasing numbers must also be regarded as tourists. In terms of sheer numbers, however, sailors, mountaineers, and environmentalists on private expeditions are now in a minority compared to the numbers of people who head southward aboard luxury ships and chartered planes.

Whether an individual is a member of a government or nongovernment party of expedition is often the basis used by countries to define who are to be classified as tourists, for they are able to exert some degree of control over government employees. But the government scientist from McMurdo Station who visits Scott's Hut on his day off should also be regarded as a tourist. Thus, if these individuals are also included in the calculation, the number of so-called "tourists" is doubled.

Greenpeace has played an important role in protecting the few remaining species of whales that live in Antarctica, and has raised the level of public awareness about Antarctic conservation. There is still much to be done, however.

Antarctic tourism has come of age. It has been over twenty-one years since the first paying passengers landed on the Antarctic Peninsula from Spanish, Italian, and Argentinian passenger liners. Visits on this scale ceased in 1977, but three specially built luxury ships, the *World Discoverer* and *World Explorer* (formerly the *Lindblad Explorer*), and the *Frontier Spirit* now conduct regular subantarctic and Antarctic cruises each southern hemisphere summer, and more ships are under construction. Most of these cruises originate in Australia, New Zealand, or South America.

Such cruises tend to be expensive, but they are also of the very highest standard. As the season during which non-icebreaking-class vessels can operate safely in ice-strewn waters is so limited, it is unlikely that shipboard Antarctic tourism will ever be drastically reduced in price.

Until 1980 an average of less than 1,000 people per year had landed in Antarctica, arriving either by plane or cruise ship. But when Chile began running flights into their bases for paying passengers, and with the advent of the cruise ships that have a capacity for some 400 passengers each, this figure is increasing rapidly. In the course of forty-five flights flown by Air New Zealand and Qantas between 1976 and 1981, nearly 11,000 sightseers were able to experience this perspective of the Antarctic. Such flights were discontinued when an Air New Zealand DC10 crashed into the slopes of Mount Erebus, killing all 275 passengers and crew. There is some renewed interest in resuming similar flights, but so far the air-safety authorities of Australia and New Zealand have denied permission, citing the lack of search-and-rescue facilities in Antarctica.

Mountaineers and adventurous sailors are as much tourists as those visiting the continent on cruise ships.

Coming face to face with penguins and seals, and experiencing the continent proper, is the pinnacle for most visitors to the Antarctic continent.

It is now possible, however, to fly to the Antarctic Peninsula and spend a day on a Chilean station, to stay in the first Antarctic hotel, or to make a guided ascent of the Vinson Massif, the highest peak in the Antarctic. There has even been a commercial skiing party to the South Pole.

The Antarctic Peninsula offers the greatest scope for tourism of this kind, followed by the Ross Sea region. Potential destinations of interest to tourists in the rest of East Antarctica are few and very widely spread. The *World Explorer* visited Mawson's Hut at Cape Denison in 1981, but an attempt to land during a later cruise was unsuccessful because of bad weather. Visits to this destination began again in 1991. As is the case at most of the Antarctic destinations, landings at these places are increasingly being controlled to minimize environmental problems.

The usual problem of policing visitors to environmentally or historically sensitive areas is nonexistent with only one form of polar tourism — the round-trip flying visitor. Commercial jumbo jets capable of flying to and from Antarctica without landing have the potential to cater to the percentage of the population that is delighted to see the Antarctic continent, if only from the air.

Though the Antarctic Treaty system recognizes tourism as a valid activity, to date there has been no attempt to provide onshore tourist facilities or to hold discussions on ways of regulating tourist activities. Some countries with a vested interest in a particular sector are beginning to try to police such behavior in their own region. New Zealand, for example, is concerned about preventing environmental damage in and around the historic huts on Ross Island and now requires cruise ships to have a suitably qualified government representative aboard.

Historic huts and monuments are a focus for ship-based tourists visiting the Antarctic, but the pristine wilderness of the Antarctic *(far right)* must be preserved for future generations.

Tourism in the Antarctic is a controversial subject in conservation and Antarctic Treaty circles. Extreme environmentalists are not in favor of any form of tourism because of the potential for ecosystems and historic sites to be disturbed. Likewise, certain treaty members object to the disruption suffered by some scientific stations by the arrival of cruise ships bearing hundreds of passengers.

It is unlikely that tourism could ever be entirely prevented, however, because the demand by travelers to experience Antarctica is steadily growing. Uncontrolled tourism may bring environmental problems to sensitive areas, yet scientists and bureaucrats ultimately depend on popular support (in the democratic world) for governments to fund their national expeditions, research, and bases. As well, carefully managed tourism could prove to be one of the most lucrative activities in the Antarctic, and if controlled it need not significantly interfere with the environment.

As the world interest in private expeditions and tourism to Antarctica increases, it seems only fair that broader sections of the community have the opportunity to experience the beauty and stimulation of the continent's spectacular scenery and wildlife.

The future of Antarctica as a pristine place, with its vast reaches of untouched country and animals that have not yet learned to be afraid of humans, is dependent on what value mankind places on the continent's various resources. It is impossible to reduce to monetary terms the value of scientific research and the ongoing existence of this last great wilderness area. The intangibles must be weighed against the continent's resources—mineral and oil deposits, fish populations, the water trapped within the icebergs, and many others. Yet, it should be remembered that, as elsewhere in the world, these resources are nonrenewable, so it is essential that the treaty nations and other interested parties determine the future of Antarctica with extreme care. They must put mechanisms in place that will ensure that the possible future exploitation of these resources will not destroy this unique continent for further scientific research, for its benefit to mankind, or for the enjoyment of future generations for whom we hold our world in trust.

Tour Operators

The major tourist operators to Antarctica are listed below. Other companies and agencies also market these tours.

In Australia:

Ausventure
P.O. Box 54
Mosman 2088
Suite 1
860 Military Rd.
Mosman Junction

Agents for Adventure Network International and subantarctic and Antarctic cruising companies.

Adventure Associates Pty Ltd
197 Oxford St.
P.O. Box 612
Bondi Junction
NSW 2022

Agents for *Salem Lindblad* Cruising that operates the MS *Frontier Spirit*.

Living Adventure
258a Rundle St.
Adelaide 5000
South Australia

Abercrombie and Kent
90 Bridport St.
Albert Park
Vic 3206

Agents for Society Expeditions who operate two ships: the *Society Explorer* (96 berths) and the *World Discoverer* (139 berths). A third ship, the *Society Adventurer,* is under construction and will be completed in June 1991.

In the United States:

Mountain Travel
6420 Fairmount Ave.
El Cerrito, CA 94530

Charters smaller cruise ships that operate in the vicinity of the Antarctic Peninsula.

Salem Lindblad Cruising Inc.
133 East 55th St.
New York, NY 10022

Operates the MS *Frontier Spirit* (164 berths). Cruises are planned in the 1990–91 summer to the subantarctic regions and the Ross Sea.

Society Expeditions
3131 Elliott Ave., Suite 700
Seattle, WA 98121

Operates two ships: the *Society Explorer* (96 berths) and the *World Discoverer* (139 berths). A third ship, the *Society Adventurer,* is under construction and will be completed in June 1991. This vessel will have a capacity of 160 passengers and will operate out of South America.

Travel Dynamics
132 East 70th St.
New York, NY 10021

Operates a passenger boat (130 berths).

In Canada:

Adventure Network International Inc.
200–1676 Duranleau St.
Vancouver, BC V6H 3S5

Adventure Network uses a DC-4 to fly into and out of the Ellsworth Mountains, where they conduct guided ascents of the Vinson Massif (Antarctica's highest mountain). The main camps are the Patriot Hills (80°S 80°W) on an ice runway, and the Thiel Mountains, a staging point on the way to the South Pole. In addition there are flights exiting Punta Arenas, Chile, by a ski-equipped Twin Otter to King George Island, and other bases and camps on the Antarctic Peninsula.

In the United Kingdom:

Society Expeditions
Albany House
324–326 Regent St.
London W1 R5AA

Antarctic Information and Conservation Organizations

In the United States:
Antarctic & Southern Ocean Coalition
1845 Calvert St. NW
Washington, D.C. 20009

The Antarctic Project
218 D St. SE
Washington, D.C. 20003

Greenpeace
1436 U St. NW
Washington, D.C. 20009

In Great Britain:
Greenpeace
Canonbury Villas
London N1 2PN

Scott Polar Research Institute
Lensfield Rd.
Cambridge CB2 1ER

World Wildlife Fund
Panda House
Weyside Part
Godalming Surrey GU7 1XR

Australasia:
Antarctic & Southern Coalition
P.O. Box 51
Balmain NSW 2041

Antarctic & Southern Ocean Coalition, New Zealand
P.O. Box 11057
Wellington, New Zealand

The Antarctic Society of Australia
Macleay Museum A12
University of Sydney
NSW 2006

Australian Conservation Foundation
340 Gore St.
Fitzroy VIC 3065

Greenpeace Australia
Studio 14, 37 Nicholson St.
Balmain NSW 2041

Greenpeace New Zealand
Private Bog
Wellesley St.
Auckland N2

New Zealand Antarctic Society
P.O. Box 1223
Christchurch, New Zealand

Suggested Reading List

Allen, K. Radway et al. *Antarctica: Great Stories from the Frozen Continent.* New York: Reader's Digest, 1985.

Bickel, Lennard. *Mawson's Will.* New York: Stern and Day, 1977.

Brewster, Barney. *Antarctica: Wilderness at Risk.* San Francisco: Friends of the Earth Books, 1982.

Huntford, Roland. *The Last Place on Earth.* New York: Atheneum Press, 1986.

May, John. *The Greenpeace Book for Antarctica: A New View of the Seventh Continent.* Toronto: Macmillan of Canada, 1988.

Mickleburgh, Edwin. *Beyond the Frozen Sea.* London: The Bodley Head, 1989.

Parfit, Michael. *South Light: A Journey to the Last Continent.* New York: Macmillan, 1985.

The Antarctic Treaty

In order to facilitate the pursuit of research in the Antarctic, and to ensure that it remained open to all nations to conduct scientific or peaceful activities there, the governments of the twelve nations who were then active in the Antarctic signed the Antarctic Treaty in Washington, D.C., on December 1, 1959. It has since been acceded to by many other nations.

The fourteen articles of the treaty may be summarized as follows:

1. Antarctica shall be used for peaceful purposes only; any military measures are prohibited.

2. Freedom of scientific investigation in Antarctica and cooperation as applied during IGY (International Geophysical Year) shall continue.

3. Plans for scientific programs and the observations and results thereof shall be freely exchanged; scientists may be exchanged between expeditions.

4. All national claims are held static from the date of signature. No future activity of any country during the life of the treaty can affect the status quo on any rights or claims to territorial sovereignty.

5. Nuclear explosions and disposal of radioactive waste are prohibited in Antarctica.

6. The provision of the treaty applies to the area south of 60°S.

7/8. Any contracting party may appoint observers. They shall have complete freedom of access at any time to any area of Antarctica, with the right to inspect any other nation's buildings, installations, equipment, ships, or aircraft or to carry out aerial observations.

9. Regular consultative meetings of the active signatory nations shall be held.

10. Contracting parties shall ensure that no activity contrary to the treaty is carried out.

11. Any disputes between contracting parties shall be resolved by peaceful negotiation, in the last resort by the International Court of Justice.

12. The treaty shall remain in force for a minimum of thirty years.

13/14. These articles provide the legal details of ratification and deposit.

In the years since the signing of the treaty, consultative meetings have reached agreement on more detailed measures, including the protection of wildlife and special areas of biological interest. Other subjects on which unanimous agreement can be reached are constantly under review. The inspections by national observers have been carried out in a spirit of friendly cooperation, and the flow of data and publications between all nations has been continuous and unrestricted.

The treaty does not apply to the high seas, nor to the subantarctic islands north of 60°S, though the latter are subject to national legislation, which, amongst other things, lays down regulations for the conservation of wildlife.

Protection of the environment and conservation of wildlife are addressed in the Agreed Measures for the conservation of Antarctic flora and fauna, which is an annex to the Antarctic Treaty of 1959. Citizens of any government that has ratified the Antarctic Treaty are legally bound by the following guidelines of conduct in the area below latitude 60°S.

Agreed Measures for the Conservation of Antarctic Flora and Fauna

Animals and plants native to Antarctica are protected under the following five instruments outlined in the Agreed Measures:

1. Protection of Native Fauna
   Within the Treaty Area it is prohibited to kill, wound, capture, or molest any native mammal or bird, or to attempt any such act, except in accordance with a permit.

2. Harmful Interference
   Appropriate efforts will be taken to ensure that harmful interference is minimized in order that normal living conditions of any native mammal or bird are protected. Harmful interference includes any disturbance of bird and seal colonies during the breeding period by persistent attention from persons on foot.

3. Specially Protected Species
   Special protection is accorded to fur and Ross seals.

4. Specially Protected Areas (SPAs)
   Areas of outstanding scientific interest are preserved in order to protect their unique nature ecological system. Entry to these areas is allowed by permit only.

5. Introduction of Nonindigenous Species, Parasites, and Diseases
   No species of animal or plant not indigenous to the Antarctic Treaty Area may be brought into the area, except in accordance with a permit. All reasonable precautions have to be taken to prevent the accidental introduction of parasites and diseases to the Treaty Area.

Antarctica Visitor's Guidelines

Visitor's Guidelines have been adopted by all the U.S. ship tour operators and are to be made available to all visitors traveling with them to Antarctica. Through such practices they will be able to operate environmentally conscious expeditions that will protect and preserve Antarctica, leaving the continent unimpaired for future generations. By doing so visitors will make an important contribution toward the conservation of the Antarctic ecosystem, and avoid potentially harmful and long-lasting damage.

1. Maintain a distance of at least 15 to 20 feet (5 to 6 m) from penguins, nesting birds, and crawling (or true) seals, and 50 feet (15 m) from fur seals. Most of the Antarctic species exhibit a lack of fear that allows you to approach closely; however, please remember that the austral summer is a time for courting, mating, nesting, and rearing young. If you approach the animals or birds too closely, you may startle and disturb them sufficiently that they will abandon the nesting site, leaving eggs or chicks vulnerable to predators. And even from the recommended distance you will be able to obtain fantastic views. You should also remember that wild animals, especially seals, are extremely sensitive to movement and a person's height above the ground in relation to their size. Approach wildlife slowly when preparing to take photographs. And it is important to remember that your photography is not over when the shutter clicks—make your retreat from the subject in the same way you approached. The key point to remember is not to cause the animals any distress. You should be careful to avoid altering their natural behavior.

2. Be alert while you are ashore! Watch your step in order not to stumble upon an aggressive fur seal or a nesting bird that is unaware of your presence. And pay attention to the behavior of flying birds as well as those on the ground. For example, when a tern or skua becomes excited or agitated and starts "dive-bombing" you, it is a good indication that you are walking too close to its nest, though you may not have spotted it.

3. Do not get between a marine animal and its path to the water, nor between a parent and its young. Never surround a single animal, nor a group of animals, and always leave them room to retreat. Animals always have the right-of-way.

4. Be aware of the periphery of a rookery or seal colony, and remain outside it. Follow the instructions given by your leaders.

5. Do not touch the wildlife. The bond between parent and young can be disrupted, and the survival of the young jeopardized.

6. Never harass wildlife for the sake of photography. Our intention is to observe wildlife in its natural state.

7. Keep all noise to a minimum in order not to stress the animals.

8. Avoid walking on, stepping on, or damaging the fragile mosses and lichens. Regeneration is extremely slow and the scars from human damage last for decades.

9. Take away only memories and photographs. Do not remove anything, not even rocks or limpet shells. This includes historical evidence of man's presence in Antarctica, such as whalebones seen at some sites that resulted from the whaling industry's activities.

10. Return all litter to the ship for proper disposal. This includes litter of all types, such as film containers, wrappers, cigarette butts, and tissues. Garbage takes decades to break down in this environment.

11. Do not bring food of any kind ashore.

12. Do not enter buildings at the research stations unless invited to do so. Remember that scientific research is going on, and any intrusion could affect the scientists' data. Be respectful of their work.

13. Historic huts can only be entered when accompanied by a specially designated government representative or properly authorized ship's leader.

14. Never smoke near wooden buildings or refuge huts. Fire is the greatest hazard in Antarctica! The wood is generally very dry and can easily catch fire, winds are usually prevalent, and fire-fighting equipment is not readily available. Please return any cigarette butts to the ship for disposal.

15. When ashore stay with the group and/or one of the ship's leaders. For your own safety, do not wander off on your own.

16. Listen to the expedition leader, lecturers, and naturalists. They are experienced and knowledgeable about Antarctica. If you are not sure about something, please don't hesitate to ask your leaders and guides.

INDEX